THE

Shabti

COLLECTIONS

THE Shabti COLLECTIONS

1

West Park Museum, Macclesfield

Glenn Janes

Foreword Alan D Hayward

Olicar House Publications • Cheshire England
www.shabtis.com

This volume is one of a series of catalogues on the *shabti* collections in museums in the north west of England

The West Park Museum is managed by the Silk Heritage Trust on behalf of Cheshire East Council. The Museum and Egyptian collections are all the property of Cheshire East Council and citations should acknowledge this.

PUBLISHER
Olicar House Publications • Cheshire England

DISTRIBUTOR
Orchard Enterprises
Orchard House • Oughtrington Lane • Lymm
Cheshire WA13 0RD
distribution@shabtis.com

Cover design: Roger Dowling
Hieroglyphs database: John Wade and Glenn Janes
Photography: Glenn Janes unless stated

ISBN 978-0-9566271-0-0

The Amadeus Press
FINE BOOK & COLOUR PRINTERS
Ezra House • West 26 Business Park • Cleckheaton
Yorkshire BD19 4TQ

Contents

Architect's watercolour and ink painting of West Park Museum by T. Roylance Lawton, Feb. 1898 - this was the final design accepted by Marianne Brocklehurst for the Museum

(*West Park Museum, Macclesfield* - 282.1976)
Photograph courtesy Alan Bardsley

Preface

DEATH and the obsessive preoccupation with life thereafter provided Egypt with one of its greatest industries. The manufacture of funerary statuettes, called *shabtis*, *shawabtis* or *ushabtis*, depending on when they were made, was a small but nonetheless essential part of it. For the sake of simplicity they are generally called *shabtis* as a category of object.

Shabtis are usually small mummy-shaped figures but some from the New Kingdom and Third Intermediate Period are dressed in the clothes of everyday life. They range in height from just a few centimetres to larger statuettes nearly 60 cm. tall but the majority are between 10 and 20 cm. They probably evolved either from small human-shaped figures placed in miniature coffins towards the end of the First Intermediate Period (2160-2040 BC), or more likely from wooden servant figures included in burials during the early Middle Kingdom (2134-1991 BC). These wooden figures disappeared with the introduction of *shabtis* which were then in use until the end of the Ptolemaic Period (332-30 BC), an overall time-span of around 2,000 years. Because of the large number produced they are among the most numerous of Egyptian antiquities.

Every museum with an Egyptian collection has *shabtis* on display and usually has a number in reserve collections. Cairo Museum has in excess of 40,000 *shabtis*.

Shabtis were made of stone (limestone, sandstone, schist, alabaster, serpentine, granite, greywacke and steatite), glass, bronze, wood (tamarisk, sycamore, acacia, ebony, cedar and perhaps persea), pottery (including sun-baked clay), wax, and most commonly faience. Glass and wax *shabtis* are extremely rare, with only a handful of examples being known. Bronze is also uncommon. *Shabtis* are generally considered to have been made in workshops attached to temples and palaces although there may have been private workshops too.

Important private persons, both male and female, as well as royalty, included *shabtis* among their burial equipment. The more important ones are invariably inscribed with the titles and names, sometimes including the parentage, of the person who had them made as part of his or her burial goods. They were regarded as substitutes for the deceased owner should they be called upon to work in the Afterlife. The work would have been of an agricultural nature - maintaining irrigation ditches and canals to water the land and enable crops to be grown and cultivated, thus providing the deceased with an everlasting supply of food. During the reign of Tuthmosis IV (1419-1386 BC) in the New Kingdom, implements comprising narrow and broad-bladed hoes, baskets, and sometimes water-pots and brick-moulds, became features modelled or painted on *shabtis* to enable the figures to carry out the specific tasks specified in the *shabti* spell, Chapter 6 of the Book of the Dead, with which many *shabtis* are inscribed.

Initially only one or two *shabtis* were placed in burials but the number gradually increased during the New Kingdom. By the Third Intermediate Period the number had risen dramatically, the ideal being 401 figures. This number included one worker *shabti* for every day of the year and 36 'overseers', one for every 10 workers. The 'overseer' *shabtis* are not mummiform but depicted as living figures. They wear the kilt of everyday life with a projecting frontal apron and carry a whip to keep the workers in order. There is a very interesting 'overseer' *shabti* in West Park Museum which has been modified from a worker (see cat. No. 5).

Shabtis were usually placed in tombs in specially made boxes. There is a particularly fine example in West Park Museum (see cat. No. 35).

Several of the *shabtis* in the collection are from two sites of particular interest at Thebes. These are known as the Royal Cache (TT 320) and the Priests of Amen Cache. They are also known as Cache I and Cache II. They are in close proximity to the memorial temple of Queen Hatshepsut at Deir el-Bahari. I have given a brief outline of the discovery of these tomb caches in this publication. In West Park Museum there are a series of watercolour sketches painted by Marianne Brocklehurst in 1891. Two of these, which are reproduced in figs. 8 and 9, give the only pictorial records of the discovery of the Priests of Amen Cache and as such are unique historical documents.

A number of other *shabtis* in the collection are from Abydos, Cemetery G, Tomb G 50. A brief account of the contents of this tomb is given under the entry for a *shabti* for Djed-Hor (see cat. No. 30).

The lists of parallel examples of *shabtis* in this catalogue are by no means comprehensive. I am naturally responsible for any omissions or errors that occur. I can be contacted by email at glennjanes@shabtis.com or via the web site www.shabtis.com for any comments or suggestions.

I hope publication of this catalogue, one of a series on *shabtis* found in some of the museums in the north west of England, will encourage others to do similar work on other objects found in these museums.

Acknowledgements

THANKS must be given to Alan Hayward, the Honorary Curator of the Egyptian collections at West Park Museum, Macclesfield for his patience during my numerous visits to photograph, measure and study the *shabtis*. I must thank the Silk Heritage Trust and its Director, Richard de Peyer for allowing me to publish this catalogue.

I would also like to thank the Curators, Collections Assistants and Documentation Officers in the many museums I visited in the search for parallel *shabtis*. Others kindly sent me information about their collections for me to study. In particular I must mention Katina Bill (Kirklees Museums & Galleries), Joanne Chamberlain (Atkinson Art Gallery, Southport), Jean-Luc Chappaz (BSEG, Geneva - author of the *Répertoire Annuel des Figurines Funéraires*), Dr Ashley Cooke (National Museums, Liverpool), Dr Karen Exell (The Manchester Museum), Tracey Golding (The Petrie Museum of Egyptian Archaeology, London), Tom Hardwick (Bolton Museum & Art Gallery), Jo Hayward (World of Glass, St. Helen's), Lesley-Ann Liddiard (National Museum of Scotland, Edinburgh), Andrew Moore (Rochdale Arts and Heritage Service), Chris Naunton (EES, London), Craig Sherwood (Warrington Museum & Art Gallery), Dr John Taylor (British Museum, London), Dr Helen Whitehouse (Ashmolean Museum, Oxford) and George Woods (McLean Museum and Art Gallery, Greenock).

Foreword

Alan D Hayward

Honorary Curator of the Egyptian Collection, West Park Museum, Macclesfield

MARIANNE BROCKLEHURST was born in 1832 at Hurdsfield House in Macclesfield. Her father John Brocklehurst had made a fortune from the silk industry and served as MP for the town from 1832. She was the youngest child in the family and had several elder brothers and a sister, Emma, who was 10 years her senior.

When Marianne was 14, Emma married John Coucher Dent, and shortly thereafter, their mother died. These two major events, occurring so close together, drastically changed her life, with Emma taking on their mother's role, and Marianne spending much time with her at Sudeley castle. Emma and her husband loved to travel around Britain and the Continent and they often took Marianne with them, so bringing to her a love for travel that lasted all her life.

Their father was keen to find a suitable husband for Marianne and she, being rather attractive as well as well connected, had several eligible young men in tow, but showed little interest in any of them. She then met Henry Coventry, who worked for John Dent, and fell in love, but her father objected strongly and Marianne broke off the engagement. Later she met Mary Booth, who became her lifelong companion and shared all her adventures from then on and MB, as Marianne liked to call herself, became the MBs.

After the Prince Regent had visited Egypt, it became most fashionable to take a trip on the Nile and the MBs started to plan such a trip, reading many books on the ancient Egyptians and the remains they had left behind. By the autumn of 1873 all was ready and they set out from Marianne's London home on Tuesday 11th November by entraining for Dover, crossing the Channel and taking a train to Paris. The week before, they had sent off a cartload of baggage ahead of them.

As well as the MBs, the party consisted of Marianne's nephew, Alfred and a footman, George, who one assumes was there to keep an eye on them all on this trip into the unknown.

After spending a few days in Paris, they took a train to Turin via the Cenis tunnel then on to Brindisi, where they were to board a ship for Alexandria. The crossing of the Mediterranean was very rough and everyone was seasick. They finally arrived at Alexandria on 27th November, but were not allowed on shore due to quarantine regulations.

It was during this voyage that Marianne met Amelia Edwards and her companion Miss Renshawe. Amelia was a successful author, writing accounts of her travels. She had been on a trip in Europe, but the weather had been so bad

Fig. 1 *Marianne Brocklehurst on Horseback* by Henry Valvert c. 1853

(West Park Museum, Macclesfield - 237.1976)
Photograph courtesy Alan Bardsley

that, on an impulse, she had decided to divert to Egypt. It was agreed at this time that they would travel the Nile together and both parties took a train for Cairo, where they settled into Shepherd's Hotel. We know a great deal about this first visit to Egypt as MB kept a diary giving many insights and Amelia Edwards wrote her most famous book about it (see Bibliography).

The main task of their stay in Cairo was in finding suitable Nile boats to take them up river, but many hours were also spent exploring Cairo and on a trip to the pyramids. After much hassle, the MBs found a suitable *dahabeeya*, which they renamed 'Bagstones,' after MB's house, while Amelia Edwards hired the 'Philae,' and on Saturday 13th December both boats set off up the Nile.

In her book on the journey, Amelia described her *dahabeeya* as ' ... shallow and flat-bottomed, adapted for sailing or rowing, with cabins on deck and a raised 'open-air drawing room.' She also thought George was special, saying: 'They had brought him, partly because he is a good shot and may be useful to master Alfred after birds and crocodiles; and partly from a well-founded belief in his general abilities. He is a fellow of infinite jest and infinite resource and takes to the Egyptian life as a duckling to the water. He picks up Arabic as if it were his mother tongue; he skins birds like a practised taxidermist; he can even wash and iron on occasion. He is in short groom, footman, housemaid, laundry maid, stroke oar, gamekeeper and general factotum all in one. And besides all this he is gifted with a comic gravity of countenance that no surprises and no disasters can upset for a moment. To see this worthy anachronism cantering along in his groom's coat and gaiters, livery buttons, spotted neckcloth, tall hat and all the rest of it; his legs dangling within an inch of the ground on either side of the most diminutive of donkeys; his double-barrelled fouling piece under his arm, and that imperturbable look on his face, one would have sworn that he and Egypt were friends of old, and that he had been brought up on pyramids from his earliest childhood.'

They soon settled into a routine, for at Memphis, shortly after setting off, the ladies spent time sketching and 'grubbing,' as they called their searches for antiquities in the sand, whilst Alfred went shooting for any game he could find. Although at this time there were still many items to be found laying around in the desert, most of the items that are now in the collection were purchased from Egyptians in the bazaars and the MBs spent a lot of time bargaining for both provisions and antiquities.

At the villages they moored near, MB would bargain with the local chief for the food for both themselves and the crew. The *dahabeeya* soon became well stocked with cocks, hens, geese, turkeys and a sheep and they called their life on board 'a Noah's Ark life,' patriarchal, pleasant and peaceful.

So they continued upstream, with the two *dahabeeyas* always together, sailing, and sometimes racing each other, when the wind was up, or dragging the boat against the current when there was no wind. Such was their anxiety to make use of the wind, when it did blow, that they passed by many places, such as Beni Hassan and its celebrated tombs, where they would have liked to moor up. Much time was spent in reading the books on ancient Egypt they had brought with them, working hard on Egyptian dynasties and they would spend time, when moored, with the other parties visiting their *dahabeeyas*. On Christmas day dinner was taken on board the 'Philae,' followed by entertainments by the crew.

They reached Luxor on 9th January 1874 and next day entertained the Consul, with the Governor and his son, discussing much about antiquities. But the wind was up and so on they went, reaching Aswan on the 15th. Here MB had to negotiate a price with the sheikh of the cataract for his help to get them up the First cataract (where now the Aswan dam blocks the river).

Whilst awaiting a propitious day for the sheikh to act, they visited Elephantine Island and the Aswan quarry where obelisks had been extracted. Then the day arrived and the ropes were attached to the 'Philae' and up the first section it was dragged, then came the turn of 'Bagstones' and the other *dahabeeyas* in the queue. After two days of toil, the cataracts were safely negotiated and they anchored at Philae, close to the beautiful temple of Isis. Here they wandered about by the light of the moon, being struck by the tranquillity and beauty of the place.

They were now in Nubia and the river changed, being scantily populated with few villages and desert right down to the banks. They continued upriver, making good progress for a couple of days, but then the wind failed and they had to drag the boat slowly on. They reached Wadi Halfeh and the Second cataract on 4th February. This was the turning point, as this cataract was not passable, so the sail was taken down and rowing became the main means of propulsion, aided by the current, now with them.

They now spent time at Abu Simbel, where Amelia Edwards decided to explore for a while and where one of her party discovered a previously unknown temple. The MBs, however, wanted to continue the return journey and so they split up, agreeing to meet again further north at Luxor.

As they made their slow way down stream they spent time crocodile hunting and shooting at vultures. When they reached Philae on 2nd March, Alfred managed to shoot and wound a local, which brought the whole village to the river bank screaming and carrying on. MB had to meet with the village chief and placated him with a small sum of money.

They descended the cataract and continued downstream, visiting various sites on the way, until they arrived at Luxor on 17th March. Here they spent time visiting the sites on both banks of the river and it is here that MB purchased a mummy, the case of which became the pride of her collection. As soon as they had got the mummy in MB's bedroom, they opened the case to discover the mummy, but MB was so worried that the special mummy smell would give her away that at the first opportunity she disposed of her by giving her a good Christian burial at a lonely spot on the bank of the river.

By the 9th April they had reached Beni Hassan, from where the MBs took the train to Cairo, leaving Alfred and George to continue down river in the *dahabeeya*, reaching Cairo on the 15th April. Here they packed all the treasures they had amassed and managed, presumably with many bribes and a little luck, to evade the customs officials looking for smuggled antiquities. MB's diary ends here.

They took train to Alexandria, from where the crates were shipped back to England. Alfred left them here, travelling to Venice, whilst the MBs bought tickets for Jaffa

Fig. 2 Marianne Brocklehurst as a mature lady c. 1880

(West Park Museum, Macclesfield - 238.1976)
Photograph courtesy Alan Bardsley

and Port Said. They spent the next months, first visiting the Holy Land, staying at Jerusalem, Damascus, Mount Carmel, the Sea of Galilee, Jericho, the Dead Sea and Nazareth.

At Beirut, they took a steamer, to Constantinople, which passed Cyprus and the Dardanelles, and from there home.

They clearly enjoyed this first visit to the region, as they returned in 1876. Details of this visit are much less known as we have only correspondence and MB's watercolours to tell us where they went. They took Johnny, Alfred's elder brother, with them on this occasion, as he was on leave from his regiment and was looking for some excitement.

The journey out followed a similar route, passing through the tunnel under Mont Cenis in Switzerland and then taking the steamer to Alexandria. The ship passed close by, or probably stopped at, Corfu, Corinth and Athens and here they must have broken their journey as they visited Marathon.

They seem to have stayed near Cairo on this visit and probably did not hire a *dahabeeya*, for we only know of them visiting Saqqara, Dashur and Giza. They did not stay at Shepherd's Hotel either, but camped out in the desert.

In February 1877, whilst at Cairo, they met up with General Gordon who was passing through to the Sudan, where he had been asked to become governor. He was eventually to meet his death there at the siege of Khartoum. MB must have known him from a previous meeting for she introduced Johnny to him and they all had dinner together. Johnny and Gordon became instant friends and Johnny left the MBs to journey up the Red Sea to Abyssinia with General Gordon.

The MBs also travelled to Suez and into the Sinai Peninsular, visiting Mount Sinai and other biblical sites and must have got really experienced at camping in the desert. They visited Akabah and Jerusalem, before returning home, one assumes by the same route as before.

The MBs next visited Egypt during the winter of 1890/91. All we know of this visit is that they visited Luxor and had Alice Booth with them. It was an exciting time as a cache of mummies had recently been found at Deir el-Bahari by a local Egyptian family, the Abd el-Rassul brothers, and the party went to Hatshepsut's temple on the West Bank to witness their being lifted out of the shaft and carried down to *dahabeeyas* on the river bank for shipment to Cairo.

These mummies were of Priests of Amun, of the Third Intermediate Period and they had been reburied without any of the valuables normally buried with the nobility, but with their shabtis to serve them. It must have been during this visit that MB acquired the *shabtis* for this period that the Egyptians had taken from the tomb prior to informing the authorities of its existence (see cat. Nos. 5 & 10).

No doubt MB added to her Egyptian collection during this visit to Cairo, but she had joined the Egypt Exploration Fund founded by Amelia Edwards, which sent archaeologists to Egypt on digs and surveys, and distributed what they had managed to bring back to the members. Many of the objects in the collection were donated to MB by the EEF. Smuggling was now not necessary as all was above board, but no doubt MB still dabbled in this whilst in Egypt just for the thrill of it.

MB was an experienced and knowledgeable Egyptologist by this time and was constantly adding to her collection and looking for objects to fill gaps in it. The collection she left, although small in quantity compared with the major collections, is a well balanced and representative sample of what has come down to us.

Towards the end of her life, she had the idea of donating a museum to her home town to house the collection and West Park Museum was the result. She was unwell, however, during the construction of this museum and last saw it as the walls were being erected. She died in London just three weeks after it was opened to the public.

In her Will she left her collection and her diary and her scrapbooks of watercolours and sketches to her great-niece, Lady Yarborough, who very kindly donated them to the museum in Macclesfield.

BIBLIOGRAPHY

A. B. Edwards, *A Thousand Miles up the Nile* (London, 1877)

A. R. David, *The Macclesfield Collection of Egyptian Antiquities* (Warminster, 1980)

M. Brocklehurst, *Miss Brocklehurst on the Nile: Diary of a Victorian Traveller* (Disley, 2004)

J. Bray, *The Mysterious Captain Brocklehurst - General Gordon's Unknown Aide*, (Cheltenham, 2006)

The Deir el-Bahari Caches

TOWARDS the end of the New Kingdom, tomb robbing was becoming increasingly troublesome in the Theban necropolis. Especially at risk were the royal burials in the Valley of the Kings. One only has to look at the wealth of treasure found in the tomb of Tutankhamen to get an idea of the valuable commodities the royal tombs held for robbers. The burials of the nobility, including those of the priesthood, were also at risk. In an attempt to ensure eternal life for the deceased, several tombs were designated as caches to hide the mummies and coffins with a limited amount of funerary equipment including *shabtis*. Because the West Park Museum, Macclesfield, has several *shabtis* originating from two of these caches it is worth giving a brief outline of their discovery and contents.

'There were whispers about this time of a tomb that had been discovered on the western side - a wonderful tomb, rich in all kinds of treasures. No one of course, had seen these things. No one knew who had found them. No one knew where they were hidden. But there was a solemn secrecy about certain of the Arabs, and a conscious look about some of the visitors, and an air of wakened vigilance about the government officials, which savoured of mystery. These rumours by and by assumed more definitive proportions. Dark hints were dropped of a possible papyrus; the M. B.'s [Marianne Brocklehurst] *babbled of mummies; and an American dahabeeyah, lying innocently off Karnak, was reported to have a mummy on board.*

Meanwhile we tried in vain to get sight of the coveted papyrus. A grave Arab dropped in once or twice after nightfall, and talked it over vaguely with the dragoman; but never came to the point. He offered it first, with a mummy, for £100. Finding, however, that we would neither buy his papyrus unseen nor his mummy at any price, he haggled and hesitated for a day or two, evidently trying to play us off against some rival or rivals unknown, and then finally disappeared. These rivals, we afterwards found, were the M. B.'s. They bought both mummy and papyrus at an enormous price; and then unable to endure the perfume of their ancient Egyptian, drowned the dear departed at the end of the week.'

Amelia Edwards, *A Thousand Miles up the Nile* (London, 1877)

The Royal Cache - Cache I (TT320)

This cache, located in the cliff face just south of the memorial temple of Queen Hatshepsut,[1] remained undiscovered until late in the nineteenth century. There are varying accounts of the discovery.[2] The most likely version says that in 1871 Ahmed Abd el-Rassul, a native of the nearby village of Qurna, stumbled across the tomb whilst he was in pursuit of one of his goats which had fallen down a partially concealed shaft which led to the cache. He was already well-experienced as a tomb robber, and after investigation he must have realised what an incredible find he had made.

Ahmed Abd el-Rassul had two brothers, Mohammad and Hussein. They managed to keep the discovery quiet and were able to sell objects from the cache on the antiquities market in Luxor for the next 10 years. The number and importance of the objects appearing for sale eventually raised suspicions, especially those of August Mariette, the Director of the Antiquities Service. He himself purchased two funerary papyri for the Boulaq Museum in Cairo in 1871 or 1872. They belonged to Queen Henut-tawy, wife of King Pinudjem I.[3] During her visit to Egypt in 1873 Marianne Brocklehurst also bought an important funerary papyrus which belonged to Djed-Ptah-iwef-ankh. This was recounted by Amelia Edwards in her famous book *A Thousand Miles up the Nile* (see panel).

What happened to the papyrus bought by Marianne Brocklehurst is a mystery as its present whereabouts is unknown.[4] It was published by both Edwards (1883) and Naville (1886).[5]

Another papyrus from the Royal Cache is that of Pinudjem II. This was bought by an English officer, Colonel Archibald Campbell in 1874. It is now in the British Museum (EA 10793).[6] These are but a few of the objects that must have appeared on the antiquities market in Luxor. Undoubtedly a number of *shabtis* were sold, being easily transportable and very attractive with their distinctive bright blue glaze. It must be assumed that Marianne Brocklehurst bought the five *shabtis* known to have been found in the Royal cache (cat. Nos. 6a-d & 9) during her visit in 1873 although there is no record of their purchase.

Eventually the finger of suspicion was pointed at the Abd el-Rassul family. Ahmed was arrested and, according to some accounts, tortured to try and gain information from him as to the whereabouts of his discovery. In 1881 Mohammed Abd el-Rassul, the eldest of the brothers, decided, for the sum of £500, to reveal his family's secret to Émile Brugsch. He was temporarily in charge of the Antiquities Service in the absence of Gaston Maspero who was Director following the death of Mariette in 1881.

Brugsch was taken to see the cache by Mohammed Abd el-Rassul. He was staggered at what he was shown.

'Soon we came upon cases of porcelain funeral offerings, metal and alabaster vessels, draperies and trinkets, until, reaching the turn in the passage, a cluster of mummy-cases came into view in such number as to stagger me.

Collecting my senses, I made best examination of them I could by the light of my torch, and at once saw that they contained the mummies of royal personages of both sexes; and yet that was not all. Plunging on ahead of my guide, I came to the chamber where we are now seated, and there standing against the walls or here lying on the floor, I found even a greater number of mummy-cases of stupendous size and weight.

Their gold coverings and their polished surfaces plainly reflected my own excited visage that it seemed as though I was looking into the faces of my own ancestors.'

Brugsch hurriedly arranged for the tomb to be cleared of its contents fearing repercussions from the locals living in the village of Qurna once they had heard of the disclosure of the cache.

'It is true I was armed to the teeth, and my faithful rifle, full of shells, hung over my shoulder; but my assistant from Cairo, Ahmed Effendi Kemal, was the only person with me whom I could trust. Any one of the natives would have killed me willingly, had we been alone, for every one of them knew better than I did that I was about to deprive them of a great source of revenue. But I exposed no sign of fear and proceeded with the work.'

E. Wilson quoting Brugsch in *The Century Magazine* (New York, 1889) vol. XXXIV no. 1

There were 40 coffins with mummies, including 20 for Kings and Queens of the New Kingdom, 10 for other royal persons, and the remainder for priests and priestesses of the Third Intermediate Period. The Kings included Amenophis I, Tuthmosis I, II and III, Ramesses I, II, III and IX, and Seti I. Coffins of the 'High Priests of Amen,' who ruled as Kings in the Third Intermediate Period, included Pinudjem I and II, and Masaharta, together with their wives. There were also a number of items of funerary equipment including at least 20 *shabti* boxes, canopic jars, bronze vessels, faience and glass cups, Osiris figures, a funerary tent, and several papyri.[7] There were also a large number of *shabtis* mainly found strewn about the floor. They all belonged to the Third Intermediate Period burials. The *shabtis* are made of faience and the majority have a brilliant blue glaze. Aubert comments that the number of *shabtis* originally found exceeded 4,000 in number and that about 300 were sold by the Abd el-Rassuls on the antiquities market.[8] Maspero, however, wrote that '*nous en avons recueilli encore plus de trois mille, dont beaucoup se sont malheureusement brisés pendant le transport.*'[9] Clayton suggests it was the appearance of the *shabtis* on the art market that initially alerted Maspero that a major find had been made.[10]

There are currently about 320 *shabtis* from the Royal Cache on display in Cairo Museum but it is not known whether the museum has others in reserve collections.

It took just two days to empty the tomb with the help of Brugsch's assistants and some 300 local men. Within two weeks the coffins etc. were sent aboard the Khedive of Egypt's boat to the museum at Bulaq. A great oversight in archaeological terms is the fact that the clearing of the cache and its important contents was never recorded. No photographs were taken and no on-the-spot details were noted. A number of the coffins and mummies were mixed up, probably by the Abd el-Rassuls in their attempt to search for the more interesting and valuable objects.

It is of interest to recount the writings of Robert de Rustafjaell, a British/American collector and author, who met Ahmed Abd el-Rassul some 38 years after the discovery of the cache.

'In 1871, Abd-el Rassul Ahmed Abd-el Rassul, native of Thebes, discovered a shaft near the foot of the mountain at Dêr-al-Baharî. When opened up, he found it led into a gallery and a set of subterranean chambers, containing the most important find ever made in Egypt of priceless treasures and about thirty coffins with royal cartouches. These turned out to be the mummies, amongst others, of Kings Aahmes, Thotmes I, II, and III, Rameses I, II, and III, and Seti, now in Cairo Museum. The finder was imprisoned and flogged, but later set free.

He will be seen in Plate XXVII [Fig. 3], *seated near the mouth of the shaft itself. The day this view was photographed, Abd-el Rassul conducted the writer to the shaft, and was so overcome with emotions and memories of the event itself that he fainted, and it was with great difficulty that he was propped up sufficiently to be taken. It was his first visit since the great event, when he cleared the shaft and opened up the passage, which led into the subterranean chambers, thirty-eight years ago.*

He is still alive, and nearly ninety years old, and dependant on charity; his mother died a few months ago at the age of 120. Her picture will be seen in the centre of the group in Plate XXIX [Fig. 4], *where four generations of the Abd-el Rassul family are portrayed, viz. his mother, Fendia, in the middle, he himself on her left, and his daughter and granddaughter on the right-hand side of the old lady. The group was taken in front of an Eighteenth Dynasty tomb at Thebes, occupied by his family and their ancestors since the twelfth century.'*

Robert de Rustafjaell, *The Light of Egypt from Recently Discovered Predynastic and early Christian Records* (London, 1909)

The history of the cache and all those buried within has been the focus of much discussion, most notably by Niwinski,[11] Reeves[12] and Forbes.[13] It is generally agreed the tomb was intended for the 'High Priest,' Pinudjem II of the 21st Dynasty and members of his family. Reeves suggests the New Kingdom royal mummies were taken to the tomb around year 11 of Sheshonq in the 22nd Dynasty, perhaps coinciding with the burial of the last member of Pinudjem's family, Djed-Ptah-iwef-ankh. It seems the New Kingdom royals were initially stored in another tomb, perhaps serving as a temporary cache, that had belonged to Queen Ahmose-Inhapy (WN A) of the 17th Dynasty. Niwinski, however,

Fig. 3 Ahmed Abd el-Rassul sitting at the entrance to the Royal Cache in 1906

Robert de Rustafjaell, *The Light of Egypt from Recently Discovered Predynastic and early Christian Records* (London, 1909) plt. XXVIII

Fig. 4 Ahmed Abd el-Rassul (right), with his mother Fendia (middle), daughter and granddaughter (left)

Robert de Rustafjaell, *The Light of Egypt from Recently Discovered Predynastic and early Christian Records* (London, 1909) plt. XXIX

suggests that some mummies, those of Ramesses I and II, and Seti I, were buried on the same day as Pinudjem II himself, and that on subsequent openings of the cache, when other members of Pinudjem's family were buried, more mummies were taken to the cache.

An interesting note is found in the diary of Marianne Brocklehurst where she describes 'How We Got Our Mummy.' She describes meeting an Arab family to discuss the purchase of a mummy and a papyrus. Could this have been the Abd el-Rassul's?

'... the M. B.s riding among the ruins of Thebes were hailed by a friendly call of 'Hie there, Bagstones,' proceeding from a tent in which sat the artist hard at work and not a hundred and fifty miles off as they had thought. The result was a halt, a chat, the leg of a chicken and a glass of Bourdeaux, and the sun going down and the donkey boys being disposed of in another direction, we stole off through the fields of ripening barley and little peas and scrambled in the dark up the rocky hill above those noble ruins which stand upon the desert to the house - or rather tomb, for rock-cut tomb it was - where the Arab family in question resided. A series of chambers cut in the solid rock and running deep into the hill, where the old hieroglyphs showed in places through the modern plaster and mud, was the rendezvous.'

Further on she writes:

'Afterwards, we were left to our own devices and had many secret interviews with the proprietors. Again we visited the den, this time to see a fine papyrus which finally was included in the bargain - first price was a hundred pounds for the two! But now we got entangled with another Arab who wished to act as a go between and have a finger in the profits and whom we had reason afterwards to suspect of treachery, of informing against us to a man in authority, but I think we propitiated both by a present of champagne and cognac and by purchasing some doubtful antiques at a good price.'

Miss Brocklehurst on the Nile - Diary of a Victorian Traveller in Egypt (Disley, 2004)

Eigner comments that the Abd el-Rassul family used an old tomb dating from the Late Period as their home (TT 390 for Irt-ieru),[14] contradicting the account by Rustafjaell. The tomb is situated in the cemetery known as the Southern Asâsîf and is very close to the Ramesseum, perhaps the 'noble ruins' mentioned in Marianne Brocklehurst's account. It was perhaps here that Marianne purchased some of her antiquities, including the five *shabtis* from the Royal Cache during her visit in 1873.

Fig. 5 The author standing at the entrance to the Royal Cache (TT 320) in 2009

Fig. 6 The shaft leading to the Royal Cache

The Priests of Amen Cache - Cache II (known as Bab el-Gusus - 'Gate of the Priests')

In January 1891 Mohammed Abd el-Rassul, brother of Ahmed Abd el-Rassul who 'discovered' the Royal Cache, was now a member of the Antiquities Service. He advised Eugène Grébaut, the Director of the Antiquities Service who was clearing part of Queen Hatshepsut's memorial temple at Deir el-Bahari, that he had found what he thought might be a tomb just outside the north-eastern corner of the temple precinct.[15] Eventually, after removing much debris used to hide the tomb and to prevent easy access for potential tomb robbers, the tomb was uncovered. It was another major discovery containing 153 coffins, 110 *shabti* boxes containing numerous *shabtis* (perhaps as many as 20,000),[16] 77 Osiris statues with many containing funerary papyri, 8 wooden *stelae*, 8 statues of Isis and Nephthys, and 16 canopic jars.[17] All the contents belonged to the Priests of Amen and their families who lived at Thebes during the Third Intermediate Period, 21st Dynasty. The *shabtis* are mostly made of faience with a light blue glaze.

Niwinski considers the tomb was built specifically for the purpose of the huge scale reburial of the Priests and their families in the 21st Dynasty. Their original tombs were undoubtedly targets for tomb robbers, so the Priests' contemporaries probably instigated the building of the cache. It is a large tomb, comprising two long adjacent corridors, some 90 m (295 ft) and 50 m (164 ft) in length, and two small rectangular burial chambers.[18] The shaft leading down to the cache was 14 m (46 ft) deep. It would have required a lot of effort to clear and refill the shaft if the burials were staggered in any way, so it seems likely that the installing of the contents in the cache was done in one single operation. If this were the case it must have taken an incredible amount of organising. Perhaps the whole procedure was spread over several consecutive days. Niwinski suggests the installing of coffins and the rest of the funerary equipment was embarked upon between 958 and 945 BC as the latest chronological evidence found on some of the mummies date from the reign of king Psusennes II.

It appears that the coffins and other objects associated with the 'High Priest,' Men-Kheper-Re were the first to be introduced to the tomb as these were found in the burial chambers cut at the end of the main corridor. The two long corridors were then filled with the remaining coffins. These were arranged along the walls to allow room for the bearers of the coffins to move. Several coffins were placed on top of each other. Those placed near the entrance of the tomb were in a state of some disarray, perhaps evidence of the haste or urgency with which the project was completed. It is a credit to the instigators of the cache that it remained undiscovered until the late nineteenth century.

Georges Daressy, the young assistant to Grébaut, was responsible for clearing and cataloguing the find. He drew up lists of the owners of the coffins and also of the owners of

Fig. 7 The Priests of Amen Cache (foreground) in front of Queen Hatshepsut's memorial temple at Deir el-Bahari (2009)

shabtis. Of the latter some 58 names were noted.[19] The cache was cleared of it contents in an operation which began on February 5th 1891 and ended on February 13th. Perhaps this timescale gives an idea of the number of days required when the cache was filled with its contents.

Of particular interest in West Park Museum are two watercolour sketches, painted in 1891 by Marianne Brocklehurst. As far as the author is aware these are the only pictorial records that show the clearing of the tomb. In this respect they are particularly valuable historical documents.

The first watercolour (Fig. 8) shows a number of coffins lying on the ground that have been removed from the cache and are awaiting transport to the Nile where they will be placed onboard a boat and taken to Cairo. One coffin is being carried by three men, either about to be moved down to the Nile or about to be laid on the ground with the other coffins that have been taken from the cache. The entrance to the cache has a winch positioned above it for hauling up the coffins which are steadied by means of ropes. Several workmen are shown winching and steadying a coffin as it appears above the ground. Another coffin is being carried by five workers away from the opening. Watching the proceedings is a figure wearing a black jacket, trousers and fez who is noted in the margins of the painting as M. Bouriant. This is Urbain Bouriant, a French Egyptologist who worked with Maspero, founder of the Mission Archéologique in Cairo in 1881. Maspero was in France at the time of the discovery of the cache so presumably Bouriant was called upon by Grébaut to assist with the clearance of the cache together with Daressy. It can be assumed Daressy and Grébaut were directing operations from inside the cache. Alongside Bouriant is Achmed Effendi and M. I. Booth. Three ladies are shown, although in outline only, standing and watching the proceedings at the front right of the painting. They are noted as MB [Marianne Brocklehurst], Alice Booth and Mary Musters. To the left of the scene are 'our donkeys, Canon Taylor, his wife and daughter.'

The second watercolour (Fig. 9) shows a long procession of Arabs carrying a number of coffins to *dahabeeyahs* moored on the banks of the Nile ready for transporting them to Cairo. It appears that each coffin needed between ten and twelve men to carry it. To accommodate this number of men the coffins are carried on long poles. A soldier on a white horse is guarding the procession with his sword held before him. Several Arabs are standing watching, including women with water jars on their heads. Luxor Temple is seen on the far bank of the Nile.

Fig. 8 'Winding up the mummy cases and mummies of priests and priestesses of Amon (XXIst Dynasty) found hidden in a vault 40 feet below the surface near Der el Bahari, Thebes 1891, M. Bouriant superintending'

(*West Park Museum, Macclesfield* - 343.118)
Photograph courtesy Alan Bardsley

Fig. 9 'Arabs carrying the mummies (140 cases) to the Nile for transportation by dahabeeiahs to Cairo'

(*West Park Museum, Macclesfield* - 343.119)
Photograph courtesy Alan Bardsley

1. For a map see Porter & Moss 1964, plt. V; Niwinski 1988, p. 205 Table IV
2. A very detailed account is given by Forbes 1998, pp. 17-57
3. Niwinski 1989, p. 54. See also pp. 265 & 269-270 (Cairo 36 and 47)
4. *ibid*, p. 54. See also p. 377 (Location Unknown 1)
5. Edwards 1883, pp. 86-87 and Naville, 1886 p. 68 no. 1
6. Niwinski 1989, p. 54. See also p. 339 (London 63)
7. For a list of the main finds see Reeves 1990, pp. 200-203 Table 3
8. Aubert and Aubert 1974, p. 141; Aubert 1974, p. 138
9. Maspero 1883, p. 329
10. Clayton 1994, p. 177
11. Niwinski 1984, pp. 73-81
12. Reeves 1990, pp. 183-192
13. Forbes 1998, pp. 16-57
14. Eigner 1984, pp. 34, 48-49, plan 17 & Tafel 26A-C; Porter & Moss 1960, pp. 440-441, map VI. The tomb is currently being restored as part of the South Asasif Conservation Project - see Pischikova 2009, pp. 38-39
15. For a map see Porter & Moss 1964, plt. V; Niwinski 1988, p. 205 Table IV
16. Berman & Bohac 1999, p. 355
17. For a general inventory see Porter & Moss 1960, pp. 630-642
18. For more on the cache, including a plan showing the positions of the coffins see Niwinski 1988, pp. 25-27 and Table 1; Lipinska 1993-94, pp. 52-53
19. Daressy 1907, pp. 3-38

Note to the Reader

The catalogue comprises 48 *shabtis*, arranged in chronological order, and a *shabti* box. Most of the *shabtis* are discussed in separate entries. These discussions are cross-referenced by catalogue and page number. All the accompanying illustrations are shown at life-size with the exception of the *shabti* box (cat. No. 35) which is reduced.

The ancient Egyptian chronology used in this catalogue is based on P. A. Clayton, *Chronicles of the Pharaohs - The Reign-by-Reign Record of the Rulers and Dynasties of Ancient Egypt* (London, 1994).

In the headings of catalogue entries, dimensions are abbreviated as follows: height (H.), width (W.), depth (D.) and length (L.).

All source references are cited in abbreviated form. Complete citations will be found in the bibliography. A list of abbreviations used in the catalogue is given before the bibliography.

Catalogue

1

MUSEUM No.	NAME(S) & TITLE(S)	DATE	MATERIAL	SIZE (cm)	PROVENANCE
1894.1977[1]	[Amenophis III]	New Kingdom, 18th Dynasty	Wood, traces of gesso and paint	Head H. 10.2 W. 2.7 D. 0.8 Hand H. 4.2 W. 2.2 D. 0.7	Unknown [probably from Thebes, Valley of the Kings, West Valley, WV 22 (or KV 22)][2]

DESCRIPTION

Although only a fragment, this face is probably from a *shabti* for Amenophis III. Several similar faces were discovered by Howard Carter who cleared the tomb of Amenophis III in 1915.[3] These are now in the collections at Highclere Castle and London, British Musuem (see below). The face appears to have been attached to the head by means of a dowel. The king wears a crown with a large *uraeus*, a symbol of Kingship, at the front; the crown is worn low on the forehead; the chin sports a long divine beard; the eyes, nose and gently smiling mouth are sensitively modelled in the carving and represent an idealized portrait of the King; several of the faces at Highclere Castle would originally have had inlaid eyes, probably of coloured glass; the front of the Macclesfield fragment has traces of gesso suggesting the face was originally painted; traces of paint remain around the eyes.

The lightly clenched hand is well-modelled. It may be from the same figure but unfortunately it is not known if the face and hand were acquired together. Despite being recorded under the same museum number there is a distinct possibility that the two pieces are unrelated.

PARALLELS

The *shabtis* for Amenophis III are found in a variety of materials including alabaster, granite, haematite, serpentine, steatite, faience and wood. They are well-documented and recorded, most recently by Bovot.[4] Parallel wooden faces are found in Highclere Castle (H57-H61, H63 and H65-66)[5] and London (BM EA 71386 - from Highclere Castle no. H62).[6]

1. David 1980, p. 58 no. H5 and illustration
2. Porter & Moss 1964, pp. 547-550
3. Reeves & Taylor 1992, pp. 125-126
4. Bovot 2003a, pp. 38-39; Janes 2002, pp. 33-36
5. Reeves 1989, p. 27 fig. 25; Reeves & Taylor 1992, p. 125
6. Communication with Dr John Taylor

2

MUSEUM No.	NAME(S) & TITLE(S)	DATE	MATERIAL	SIZE (cm)	PROVENANCE
1834.1977[1]		New Kingdom, 19th-20th Dynasty	Pottery, polychrome decoration	H. 15.0 W. 4.6 D. 3.4	Unknown

DESCRIPTION

Mummiform *shabti* wearing a tripartite wig which has traces of black paint; the front lappets are boldly modelled; the arms are crossed on the chest and the hands hold a pair of hoes although these are only just discernable in the modelling; beneath each hand is a small basket, also very faintly modelled in low relief; the upper chest appears to be painted yellow and may have been decorated with a *wesekh*-collar; the face is painted red but the features are rather worn; the body of the *shabti* has traces of white paint; the lower legs and feet are missing; there are very faint traces of horizontal register lines across the front of the body that indicate the *shabti* was originally inscribed.

1. David 1980, p. 48 no. D26 and illustration

3

	MUSEUM No.	NAME(S) & TITLE(S)	DATE	MATERIAL	SIZE (cm)	PROVENANCE
a	1835a.1977[1]		New Kingdom, 19th-20th Dynasty	Pottery, polychrome decoration	H. 15.1 W. 3.9 D. 4.1	Unknown
b	1835b.1977[1]				H. 14.4 W. 4.0 D. 2.6	
c	1836a.1977[1]				H. 13.6 W. 3.4 D. 3.5	
d	1836b.1977[1]				H. 14.9 W. 3.6 D. 4.0	

1835a.1977

1835b.1977

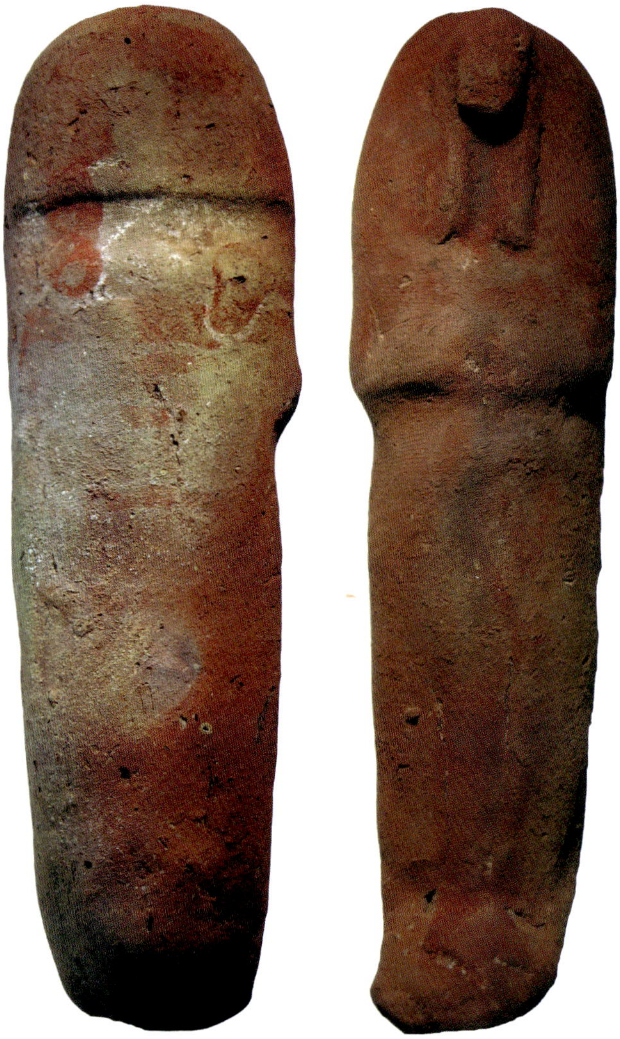

1836a.1977

1836b.1977

DESCRIPTION

A group of four mummiform *shabtis* with virtually identical iconography; especially noticeable is the very small head on each *shabti* which is completely disproportionate to the rest of the body; a plain tripartite wig is worn with front lappets in proportion to the small head; the rear lappet however, extends across the width of each figure, the bottom of the wig being indicated in the modelling; the arms are crossed on the chest but there is no suggestion of hands or implements; the upper part of the *shabtis* are painted red at the front and have a broad vertical red line extending down to the feet which are curled; the red line is less evident on 1836a.1977; large baskets are crudely painted in red on the back of the *shabtis*, although this is less visible on 1836a.1977; there are faint fingerprint marks on the front of the figures suggesting the surface was smoothed before firing.

1. David 1980, p. 48 nos. D27a, D27b, D28a & D28b - the latter are both illustrated

4

MUSEUM No.	NAME(S) & TITLE(S)	DATE	MATERIAL	SIZE (cm)	PROVENANCE
1837.1977[1]	Irt-Amen (*Ỉrt-Ỉmn*)[2] 'Ruler of Hathor' (*ḥḳ3-B3t*)	Third Intermediate Period, 22nd-23rd Dynasty	Faience, brilliant blue glaze	H. 4.4 W. 1.2 D. 1.0	Unknown

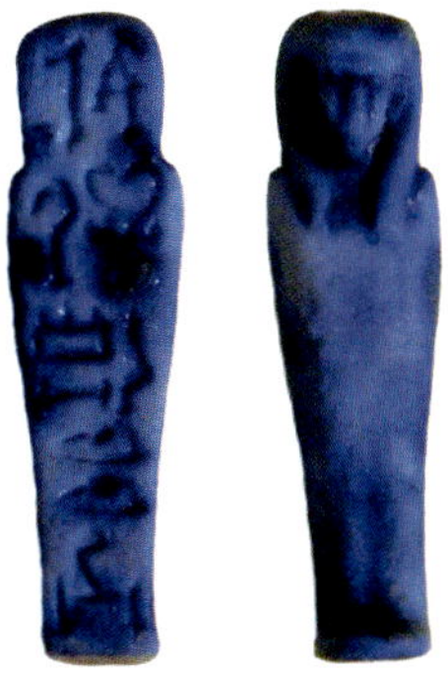

DESCRIPTION

Mummiform *shabti* wearing a plain tripartite wig; the arms, hands and implements are not indicated; the legs are slightly modelled; the back of the *shabti* is flat and has a vertical column of incised inscription; the owner is named Irt-Amen; the title 'Ruler of Hathor' (*ḥḳ3-B3t*) is unusual and seemingly quite rare.[3]

Bat was an early bovine goddess depicted with a human head, bovine ears and inward curling horns. Her image is found on the Narmer Palette (Cairo JE 32169)[4] dating from the Predynastic Period. It is also found in Old Kingdom tomb reliefs of Khwfw-Kha'f, Tiy, Khenw, 'Ankhm'ahor and Khentika where the image is worn as a pendant.[5] The emblem also occurs as the fetish in the standard of the 7th Nome of Upper Egypt. Bat had an important influence on the cult of the goddess Hathor. By the Middle Kingdom her identity and attributes had been subsumed by Hathor.[6]

INSCRIPTION

Mr nṯr ḥḳ3-B3t Ỉrt-Ỉmn m3ʿt-ḫrw

'Beloved of the God,' the 'Ruler of Hathor,' Irt-Amen, justified.

PARALLEL

There is a parallel in London (UC 13211).[7]

1. David 1980, p. 48 no. D29 and illustration
2. Ranke 1935, PN I p. 42.9 for similar
3. For the title see Faulkner 1981, p. 77. Faulkner cites Blackman 1924, p. 6 and Newberry 1893, p. 17 (nb misprint - should be p. 12). See also Erman & Grapow 1926-63, I p. 416
4. Saleh & Sourouzian 1987, pp. 43-44 no. 8
5. Badaway 1978, p. 29, fig. 38 and plt. 50
6. Wilkinson 2003, p. 172
7. Petrie Museum website

5

MUSEUM No.	NAME(S) & TITLE(S)	DATE	MATERIAL	SIZE (cm)	PROVENANCE
1810.1977[1]	Ankh-ef-en-Mut (*ʿnḫ.f-n-Mwt*)[2] 'God's Father (of) Amen and Mut' (*it-nṯr* (*n*) *Imn n Mwt*)	Third Intermediate Period, 21st Dynasty	Pottery, traces of black paint	H. 12.8 W. 3.6 D. 3.0	From Thebes, Deir el-Bahari, Cache II (the Priests of Amen Cache)[3] Acquired at Thebes in 1891

DESCRIPTION

'Overseer' *shabti* wearing a triangular apron; the figure has been modified from a worker *shabti* as is evident by the fact that it has three arms - two are crossed on the chest, as is the norm on worker *shabtis*, and the other hangs down by the right side as found on 'overseer' *shabtis*;[4] the right hand which is crossed on the chest holds a hoe modelled in shallow relief, while the one that would have been similarly indicated in the left hand has been covered by a pottery sleeve applied to the right upper arm and shoulder during the modification; the *shabti* wears a tripartite wig as worn by workers - 'overseer' *shabtis* normally wear a bi-partite wig; the eyes are outlined in black; the triangular apron, the right arm and sleeve have clearly been applied to the original worker *shabti* during the modification; there is no sign of a whip, the normal attribute of 'overseer' *shabtis*; the kilt has a vertical column of inscription in raised relief; the owner is named Ankh-ef-en-Mut.

The inscription would have been applied with a stamp before the figure was fired. This technique, which leaves the inscription in raised relief, is rarely used on *shabtis*. The inscription is read from left to right. This is the same on other known 'overseer' *shabtis* for Ankh-ef-en-Mut which also have inscriptions in raised relief. These are in Lisbon (SGL: 2507-34B)[5] and London (UC 40022).[6] Worker *shabtis* have the inscription incised into the front and it is read from right to left. It is worth noting the unusual slant of the 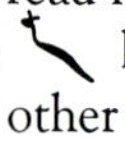 hieroglyph. This alignment is also found on a number of other examples, both workers and 'overseer' figures.

The *shabti* is from the Priests of Amen Cache, Cache II at Thebes, Deir el-Bahari (see pp. xi-xii). It was acquired at Thebes (Luxor) in 1891.

The coffins of Ankh-ef-en-Mut are in Cairo (outer coffin CG 6092 (case) & 6093 (lid) - usurped from Tchent-meri-pa-Re; inner coffin CG 6091 (lid) & 6095 (case); mummy cover CG 6094 - usurped from Pa-di-Amen).[7] His funerary papyri are also in Cairo (S.R.VII.10274 and S.R.VII.10652).[8]

Ankh-ef-en-Mut was a son of the Theban 'High Priest,' Men-Kheper-Re.[9]

INSCRIPTION

Wsir it-nṯr (n) Ỉmn n Mwt ꜥnḫ.f-n-Mwt mꜣꜥ-ḫrw

The Osiris, the 'God's Father (of) Amen and Mut,' Ankh-ef-en-Mut, justified.

PARALLELS

Parallel *shabtis* are found in Amiens (M.P. 88.3.168),[10] Basel (III 615),[11] Berlin (11948, 11949),[12] Cairo (CG 48160-48169),[13] Copenhagen (3947),[14] Cortona (89),[15] Dublin (1892:248),[16] Florence (8536. D.),[16] Leiden (F 93/10.23 & 24),[18] Lisbon (SGL: 2507-34A & SGL: 2507-34B - an 'overseer'),[19] London (BM EA 24807, 24808 & 55361;[20] UC 40021 & 40022 - an 'overseer'),[21] Marseille (5190),[22] Paris (E 22075 & E 22076),[23] Roanne (288),[24] Rome (19252),[25] St. Gallen (C 730.34),[26] St. Petersburg (4732),[27] Tubingen (1785),[28] Uppsala (18),[29] Vienna (ÄS 6190)[30] and Zurich (1093).[31] A *shabti* was in the former Michel Philippe collection.[32] An example is known in a private collection and a further *shabti* was offered for sale recently on the Internet.[33]

1. David 1980, p. 45 no. D2 and illustration
2. Ranke 1935, PN I p. 67.8
3. Daressy 1907, pp. 13, 15 & 36, List A no. 140
4. For a discussion on the modifications see Stewart 2000, pp. 166-167
5. Araújo 2003, p. 684 no. 86
6. Petrie 1935, p. 15 and plts. XVI and XL no. 435.
7. Niwinski 1988, pp. 130-131 no. 140; Niwinski 1996, pp. 126-134, plts. XXII.2; Aston 2009, pp. 190-193 TG 813
8. Niwinski 1989, pp. 289-290 (Cairo 103 & 105)
9. Naguib 1990, p. 268 no. 18. For the genealogy of Ankh-ef-en-Mut *ibid*, p. 180 and Niwinski 1988, pp. 206-207 (Ankh-ef-en-Mut C). For a different version see Dodson & Hilton 2004, pp. 200-201 & 205 (Ankh-ef-en-Mut B) in which the authors suggest Herihor as being the father
10. Perdu & Rickal 1994, p. 72 no. 94
11. Schlögl & Brodbeck 1990, p. 151 no. 90a
12. Roeder 1924, p. 320
13. Newberry 1930-57, vol. 1 pp. 298-299 and vol. 3 plt. XLIV for no. 48169
14. Mogensen 1918, p. 68
15. Botti 1955, p. 71
16. Global Egyptian Museum web site
17. Pellegrini 1900, p. 14 no. 70
18. Schneider 1977, vol. 2 pp. 142-143 nos. 4.5.1.1 & 4.5.1.2 and plt. 117, vol. 3 plt. 54
19. Araújo 2003, pp. 602, 684 nos. 8 and 86
20. Communication with Dr John Taylor
21. Petrie 1935, p. 15 and plts. XVI and XL nos. 434 & 435
22. Noted by Aubert 1998, p. 55
23. *ibid*, p. 55; for E 22075 see Aubert 1987, pp. 142-143 no. 25
24. Gabolde 1990, pp. 107-108, fig. 8 no. 89
25. Grenier 1996, p. 26 and plt. XII no. 31
26. Schlögl & Brodbeck 1990, p. 151 no. 90b
27. Noted by Aubert 1998, p. 55
28. Brunner-Traut & Brunner 1981, p. 279
29. Sandman 1930, p. 101 no. 18
30. Reiser-Haslauer 1991, pp. 82-83
31. Schlögl & Brodbeck 1990, p. 150 no. 90
32. Aubert 1998, pp. 55 & 108 no. 6 and plt. III
33. Helios Gallery

6

	MUSEUM No.	NAME(S) & TITLE(S)	DATE	MATERIAL	SIZE (cm)	PROVENANCE
a	1846.1977[1]	Kha-Kheper-Re (*Ḫꜥ-Ḫpr-Rꜥ*)[2] Pinudjem I (*P3-nḏm*)[3]	Third Intermediate Period, 21st Dynasty	Faience, bright blue glaze, details added in black	H. 13.9 W. 4.4 D. 3.3	From Thebes, Deir el-Bahari, Cache I (TT 320 - the Royal Cache)[4]
b	1847.1977[1]	'King' (*nsw*)			H. 14.1 W. 4.4 D. 3.2	
c	1848a.1977[1]				H. 14.4 W. 4.5 D. 3.0	
d	1848b.1977[1]			brilliant deep blue glaze, details added in black	H. 13.7 W. 4.6 D. 3.2	

1846.1977 1847.1977

DESCRIPTION

A group of four mummiform *shabtis* each wearing a tripartite wig with striations added in black; the rear lappet on 1846.1977 is quite short, finishing at the neck; the *shabtis* have a *uraeus* modelled in low relief on the forehead; the arms are crossed right over left on the chest and each hand holds a hoe added in black; a *wesekh*-collar incorporating drop-shaped beads is worn across the chest; the face on the *shabtis* show good detail, particularly 1848a.1977 which is quite exceptional; they all have eyes and brows added in black; each chin has a stubby beard also painted black; there is a vertical column of inscription on the front of the

1848a.1977

1848b.1977

shabtis. 1848a.1977 and 1848b.1977 are inscribed with the birth name (nomen) Pinudjem (King Pinudjem I), while 1846.1977 and 1847.1977 give the throne name of the king (prenomen) Kha-Kheper-Re.

The *shabtis* are from the Royal Cache, Cache I (TT 320) at Thebes, Deir el-Bahari (see pp. vi-ix). They were probably purchased by Marianne Brocklehurst in 1873.

Pinudjem was a 'High Priest of Amen' at Thebes who assumed the title of King and ruled over Upper and Middle Egypt. He was the third 'High Priest of Amen' to exercise his authority following a period of instability at the end of the New Kingdom. At the time of Pinudjem I, Lower Egypt, with a capital at Tanis, was ruled by King Smendes I. The two factions seemingly ruled their respective areas without conflict, perhaps having organised a power-sharing agreement.

Pinudjem I's name appears in the temple of Amen at Karnak, most notably on the processional avenue of ram-headed cryosphinxes leading to the first pylon, and those in the first courtyard which were displaced from their original position along the processional route. The cryosphinxes were usurped from Ramesses II. Pinudjem I also usurped a colossal statue of Ramesses II in front of the second pylon. His name is also found on the entrance pylon of the temple of Khonsu in the south western corner of the Karnak temple complex. Pinudjem I married Henut-tawy, a daughter of Ramesses XI. One of their daughters was the 'God's Wife of Amen,' Maat-ka-Re (see cat. No. 9).[5]

The mummy of Pinudjem I, which was found in a massive coffin for Queen Ahotep I of the 17th Dynasty (CG 61006),[6] was photographed by Brugsch soon after its discovery in the Royal Cache (TT320) in 1881.[7] The mummy was unwrapped in Cairo shortly afterwards, but its current whereabouts is unknown. His original coffin has not been identified although it is known that he usurped one made for Tuthmosis I (CG 61025).[8] Pinudjem's original coffin was either destroyed by robbers or perhaps misplaced during the hurried clearance of the Royal Cache at Thebes. There are 2 *shabti* boxes in Cairo Museum (JE 26253A & B) although 6 have been recorded.[9] A funerary papyrus is also in Cairo (S.R.VII.11488).[10]

Pinudjem I had several types of *shabtis*. There are tall worker *shabtis* with the cartouche either containing the throne name Kha-Kheper-Re (1846.1977 & 1847.1977), or the birth name (nomen) Pinudjem with the epithet 'Beloved of Amen' (1848a.1977 & 1848b.1977). There are also smaller worker *shabtis*, those with wigs that have striations shown perpendicular at the front, and rather squat examples with horizontal striations across the front of the wig. Finally there are 'overseer' *shabtis*, some of which are particularly well-modelled.

INSCRIPTION

Sḥḏ Wsir nsw Ḫꜥ-Ḫpr-Rꜥ r ir k3t nb

The illuminated one, the Osiris, the 'King,' Kha-Kheper-Re, to do all works.

1846.1977 and 1847.1977

Sḥḏ Wsir nsw P3-nḏm mry'Imn r ir k3t nb

The illuminated one, the Osiris, the 'King,' Pinudjem, 'Beloved of Amen,' to do all works.

1848a.1977 and 1848b.1977

PARALLELS

Parallel *shabtis* for Pinudjem I are found in museums and private collections around the world and have been well-documented. The most recent list was compiled by Bovot.[11] A few additional examples can be added to this list - Brighton (BTNRP 281879), Edinburgh (NMS A.1966.47 - ex MacGregor collection)[12] and Manchester (6421). Several additional *shabtis* have been noticed for sale at auctions.[13] Others are known to the author in private collections in Holland (1 example)[14] and Belgium (2 examples).

1. David 1980, p. 49 nos. D38, D39, D40 & D41 - all are illustrated
2. Ranke 1935, PN I p. 264.17
3. *ibid*, PN I p. 114.10
4. Porter & Moss 1964, p. 662
5. Dodson & Hilton 2004, pp. 200-201
6. Partridge 1994, pp. 35-36
7. Forbes 1998, p. 650
8. Niwinski 1988, p. 117 no. 73; Partridge 1994, pp. 72-73; Aston 2009, pp. 223-224 TG 915
9. Porter & Moss 1964, p. 662
10. Niwinski 1989, p. 293 (Cairo 111)
11. Bovot 2003a, p. 189
12. Communication with Lesley-Ann Liddiard
13. Sotheby, Wikinson & Hodge 1911, lot 1160; Sotheby, Wilkinson & Hodge 1912, lot 361; Parke-Bernet 1970, lot 39 (an 'overseer'); Christie's 1998, lot 153; Sotheby's 1991, lot 189; Bonhams 1994a, lot 445; Christie's 1999, lot 243; Christie's 2001, lot 326; Sotheby's 2007, lot 26; Bonhams 2009, lots 44 (an 'overseer') and 54
14. Thomassen 1993, p. 35; Thomassen 2007, p. 218

7

MUSEUM No.	NAME(S) & TITLE(S)	DATE	MATERIAL	SIZE (cm)	PROVENANCE
1827.1977[1]	Pa-kharu (*Pꜣ-ḫꜣrw*)[2] 'Priest of Amen' (*ḥm-nṯr n Ỉmn*)	Third Intermediate Period, 21st Dynasty	Faience, blue glaze, details added in black	H. 11.9 W. 4.7 D. 2.6	Unknown [perhaps from Hawara][3]

DESCRIPTION

Mummiform *shabti* wearing a tripartite wig with striations added in black; the arms are crossed left over right on the chest and the hands hold a small pair of hoes modelled in low relief and painted black; there is no evidence of a basket on the back of the figure; the face is well-modelled and the details of the eyes with brows are added in black; the body of the *shabti* has three horizontal bands of inscription; the owner is named Pa-kharu.

INSCRIPTION

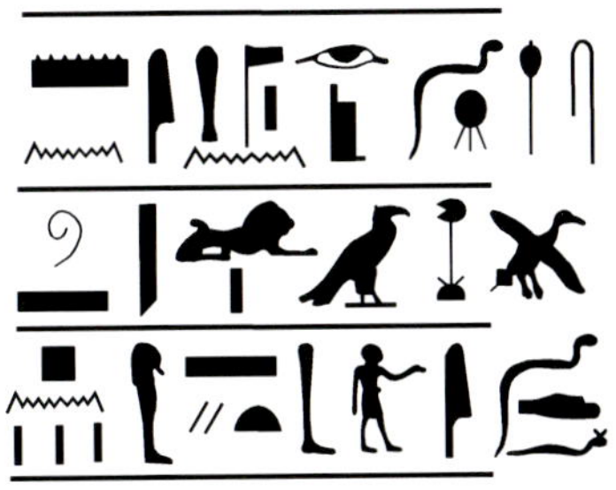

Sḥḏ Wsir ḥm-nṯr n Ỉmn Pꜣ-ḫꜣrw mꜣꜥ-ḫrw ḏd.f i šbty (i)pn

The illuminated one, the Osiris, the 'Priest of Amen,' Pa-kharu, justified, he speaks: O, these *shabtis*.

PARALLELS

Other examples are found in Cracow (XI-704)[4] and London (UC 28668).[5] An example is recorded in a private collection,[6] and a further *shabti* was offered for sale at auction.[7] It is worth noting that the example in Cracow has the title *it-nṯr* ('God's Father') in addition to *ḥm-nṯr n Ỉmn* ('Priest of Amen'). The *shabtis* in London and in a private collection have the title *it-nṯr n Ỉmn* ('God's Father of Amen').

1. David 1980, p. 47 no. D19 and illustration
2. Ranke 1935, PN I p. 116.17
3. A parallel in London (UC 28668) is recorded as coming from Hawara
4. Schlögl 2000, p. 67 no. 27
5. Petrie 1935, p. 14, plts. XVII and XXXVII no. 282
6. Janes 2002, pp. 82-83 no. 40
7. Bonhams 2009, lot 52

8

MUSEUM No.	NAME(S) & TITLE(S)	DATE	MATERIAL	SIZE (cm)	PROVENANCE
a 1843.1977[1]	Pa-di-Amenet (*P3-di-Ỉmnt*)[2]	Third Intermediate Period, 22nd Dynasty	Pottery, white paint with details added in black	H. 9.0 W. 3.4 D. 3.1	Unknown
b 1845.1977[1]				H. 9.9 W. 3.8 D. 2.9	

1843.1977

1845.1977

DESCRIPTION

Mummiform *shabtis* wearing a plain tripartite wig; the arms are crossed right over left on the chest and the hands hold a pair of small hoes indicated in shallow relief; the faces are very poorly modelled; the *shabtis* are painted white and have a vertical column of inscription added in black naming the owner Pa-di-Amenet, a female version of the name Pa-di-Amen.

INSCRIPTION

Wsir P3-di-Ỉmnt m3ʿ(t)-ḫrw

The Osiris, Pa-di-Amenet, justified.

PARALLELS

There are parallels in London (BM EA 9467 & 9468; UC 40033).[3]

1. David 1980, pp. 48-49 nos. D35 & D37 - both are illustrated
2. Ranke 1935, PN I p. 122.9
3. Petrie 1935, p. 15, plts. XI, XVII & XL no. 447

9

MUSEUM No.	NAME(S) & TITLE(S)	DATE	MATERIAL	SIZE (cm)	PROVENANCE
1850.1977[1]	Maat-ka-Re (*M3ʿt-k3-Rʿ*)[2] 'God's Wife' (*ḥmt-nṯr*)	Third Intermediate Period, 21st Dynasty	Faience, bright blue glaze, details added in black	H. 12.0 W. 4.4 D. 2.7	From Thebes, Deir el-Bahari, Cache I (TT 320 - the Royal Cache)[3]

DESCRIPTION

Mummiform *shabti* wearing a tripartite wig painted black; a *uraeus* is modelled in low relief on the forehead; immediately below the front lappets of the wig are a pair of breasts indicating this is a female worker *shabti*; well-modelled arms are crossed right over left on the chest and the hands hold a pair of hoes added in black; the face is quite broad but the chin is almost non-existent; the eyes are large with brows that almost merge into the wig; a large basket is painted in black on the back of the figure; the *shabti* is flat-backed although the arms are suggested in the modelling; there is a vertical column of inscription on the front; the owner is named Maat-ka-Re.

The *shabti* is from the Royal Cache, Cache I (TT 320) at Thebes, Deir el-Bahari (see pp. vi-ix). It was probably purchased by Marianne Brocklehurst in 1873.

Maat-ka-Re was a daughter of Pinudjem I and his principal wife Henut-tawy. Pinudjem was a 'High Priest of Amen' who assumed royal titles and ruled Upper and Middle Egypt from Thebes (see cat. Nos. 6a-d) .[4]

The mummy, coffins and other objects of Maat-ka-Re's funerary equipment are in Cairo Museum with the exception of some *shabtis*. The coffins (CG 61028)[5] comprise an outer and inner coffin together with a mummy cover. The outer coffin is particularly well-preserved with much gilding and is elaborately decorated with scenes showing Maat-ka-Re offering to various deities. The gilded face of the coffin is particularly refined. An elaborate vulture headdress covers a large wig. Three holes on the forehead once held the head of the vulture flanked by a pair of cobras, probably made of either gold or gilded wood. It is arguably the most attractive of all the coffins found in the Royal Cache.[6] The gilded face and hands on both the inner coffin and the mummy cover had been removed by tomb robbers in antiquity.[7]

The mummy (CG 61088)[8] was found in a fairly dishevelled state because ancient thieves had ripped open the mummy bandages in search of valuable jewellery.

Other objects belonging to Maat-ka-Re found in the Royal Cache were an Osiris figure (JE 46945, 46948, 46949 or 46950?)[9] which contained a funerary papyrus (Cairo S.R.IV.980; JE 26229; CG 40007),[10] a mummified baboon - probably Maat-ka-Re's pet, in its own coffin (CG 61089),[11] and two *shabti* boxes (JE 26264A-B).[12] The *shabtis* themselves were recorded as numbering 'approximately' 150 and found scattered about the floor.[13] In actuality at least 186 *shabtis* have been noted in recent work by de Haan in collaboration with the author.[14]

Maat-ka-Re is depicted on temple reliefs at Luxor and Karnak.[15] In these scenes and on her funerary objects she has a number of titles including 'King's Daughter of his body,' 'Beloved Daughter of the Great Royal Wife,' 'Great Daughter, Lady of the Two Lands,' 'Divine Adoratrice,' 'God's Wife,' 'Pure Priestess of the Two Hands of Amen of Karnak,' 'Princess,' 'Great Songstress' and 'Great Songstress of the Choir of Amen of Karnak.' As holder of the title 'God's Wife,' Maat-ka-Re was the most important lady in Thebes at the time. The 'God's Wife' was regarded as the earthly wife of the god Amen. Maat-ka-Re had a throne name (prenomen) of Mut-em-het also written in a cartouche.

Another of Maat-ka-Re's titles, 'Divine Adoratrice,' was usually synonymous with that of 'God's Wife' (see cat. No. 11). As 'Great Songstress' and 'Great Songstress of the Choir of Amen of Karnak,' she presumably communicated to the god by singing.[16]

INSCRIPTION

Sḥḏ Wsir ḥmt-nṯr nbt tȝwy
Mȝʿt-kȝ-Rʿ

The illuminated one, the Osiris, the 'God's Wife,' the 'Lady of the Two Lands,' Maat-ka-Re.

PARALLELS

Shabtis for Maat-ka-Re are found in museums and private collections around the world. There are too many parallels to list for the purposes of this catalogue. A large number have already been recorded by various authors,[17] while others are noted for future publication.[18]

1. David 1980, p. 45 no. D43 and illustration
2. Ranke 1935, PN I p. 145.7
3. Porter & Moss 1964, p. 663 no.6
4. For genealogy tables see Niwinski 1988, pp. 206-207 table 5; Naguib 1990, p. 180 - 3.6.3; Janes 2002, p. XXV
5. Daressy 1909, pp. 82-95 and plts. XXXIX-XLI; Niwinski 1988, p. 116 no. 68; Aston 2009, pp. 225-226 TG 917
6. Forbes 1998, p. 658; Tiradritti 1998, pp. 298-299
7. Partridge 1994, pp. 198-199
8. Smith 1912, pp. 98-101 and plts. LXXII-LXXIV
9. Reeves 1990, p. 201 table 3/2; Aston 2009, p. 225
10. Niwinski 1989, p. 268 (no. 43)
11. Aston 2009, p. 225
12. Porter & Moss 1964, p. 663; Aston 1994, pp. 31 and 45; Aston 2009, p. 225 where it is noted that JE 26264B was originally JE 26268. For JE 26264B see Stuart 1882, plt. 32 - opposite p. 41. The box is quaintly described as a 'casket containing mummy dolls' on p. xii; Hope 1988, pp. 66-67 no. 17
13. Gauthier 1914, p. 254
14. de Haan 2009, p. 25
15. Porter & Moss 1972, pp. 228-229 and 307
16. Manniche 1991, p. 124
17. Bovot 2003a, pp. 322-333
18. Janes, in preparation

10

MUSEUM No.	NAME(S) & TITLE(S)	DATE	MATERIAL	SIZE (cm)	PROVENANCE
1809.1977[1]	Nesy-Amen (*Nsy-Imn*)[2] 'Fourth Prophet of Amen-Re, King of the Gods' (*ḥm-nṯr 4-nw n Imn-Rᶜ nsw nṯrw*)	Third Intermediate Period, 21st Dynasty	Faience, blue glaze, details added in black	H. 12.4 W. 3.9 D. 3.3	From Thebes, Deir el-Bahari, Cache II (the Priests of Amen Cache)[3] Acquired at Thebes in 1891

DESCRIPTION

Mummiform *shabti* wearing a plain tripartite wig with a *seshed* headband added in black; the arms are crossed right over left on the chest and the hands hold a pair of hoes; the face is simply modelled and has eyes with brows added in black; a basket is carried low on the back; the body of the figure has three horizontal bands of inscription; the owner is named Nesy-Amen.

The *shabti* is from the Priests of Amen Cache, Cache II at Thebes, Deir el-Bahari (see pp. xi-xii). It is recorded as being acquired at Thebes (Luxor) in 1891.

Nesy-Amen's coffins and mummy cover are in Cairo (CG 6290-6294)[4] together with his funerary papyrus (S.R.IV.1535).[5] On these objects Nesy-Amen has other titles including 'God's Father of Amen' and 'Third Prophet of Amen-Re, King of the Gods.' A *shabti* box was in Berlin (11955) but this is recorded as being lost.[6]

INSCRIPTION

Wsir ḥm-nṯr 4-nw n Imn-Rᶜ nsw nṯrw Nsy-Imn mȝᶜ-ḫrw

The Osiris, the 'Fourth Prophet of Amen-Re, King of the Gods,' Nesy-Amen, justified.

PARALLELS

Parallels are found in Alexandria (1714, 1716, 1720 & 1723),[7] Basel (Völkerkundesmuseum 619),[8] Berlin (11955 - 2 examples),[9] Boulogne (212/2),[10] Cairo (CG 46981-47000),[11] Copenhagen (3953 & 3954),[12] Cortona (83),[13] Ivanono (A-618),[14] Leiden (F 93/10.45 & F 93/10.46),[15] Lisbon (SGL: 2507-38A & B),[16] London (BM EA 24833 & 24834;[17] UC 39877),[18] Moscow,[19] Oslo (EM 8086, 8092 & 12 1601),[20] Pittsburg (CMNH 9007-37),[21] Paris (Louvre E 22089),[22] Roanne (282),[23] Rome (25225 & 55127),[24] St. Gallen (C 730.38)[25] and St. Petersburg (3851, 3854, 4609, 6176 & 6216).[26] A *shabti* was in a museum in Bucharest but has been stolen.[27] Another *shabti is* known in a private collection.[28] A further example was sold at auction[29] and two *shabtis* have been offered for sale by dealers.[30]

1. David 1980, p. 45 no. D1 and illustration
2. Ranke 1935, PN I p. 173.19
3. Daressy 1907, pp. 13, 15 & 37, List A no. 148
4. Niwinski 1988, p. 118 no. 79; Aston 2009, p. 193 TG 821
5. Niwinski 1989, pp. 272-273 (Cairo 55)
6. Roeder, 1924, p. 455
7. Noted by Naguib 1985, p. 39
8. Schlögl & Brodbeck 1990, p. 171 no. 104a
9. Roeder 1924, p. 321
10. Noted by Aubert 1998, p. 71
11. Newberry 1930-57, vol. 1 pp. 61-64, vol. 3 p. 412 and plts. XXXIII, XXXVII & XL
12. Mogensen 1918, p. 58
13. Botti 1955, p. 73
14. Berlev & Hodjash 1998, p. 87 plt. 112 no. 30
15. Schneider 1977, vol. 2 pp. 127-128 plt. 115, vol. 3 plt. 50 nos. 4.3.1.43 & 4.3.1.44
16. Araújo 2003, pp. 630-633 nos. 36 and 37
17. Communication with Dr John Taylor
18. Petrie 1935, p. 14 and plts. XIX & XXXVII no. 275
19. Noted by Aubert 1998, p. 71
20. *ibid*, pp. 38-41
21. Patch 1990, p. 110
22. Aubert 1998, pp. 71, 124 & 126
23. Gabolde 1990, pp. 120, 285 fig. 9 no. 103
24. Grenier 1996, pp. 72-73 nos. 105 & 106 and plt. XLV
25. Schlögl & Brodbeck 1990, p. 171 no. 104
26. Noted by Aubert 1998, p.71
27. Cihó 1984, pp. 91-95; communication with M. Cihó
28. Janes 2002, pp. 92-93 no. 46 - see also Aubert 1998, pp. 71, 109, plt. X
29. Bonhams 1994b, part of lot 229B
30. Ede 1989, no. 44; Eternal Egypt 1990, no. 16

11

MUSEUM No.	NAME(S) & TITLE(S)	DATE	MATERIAL	SIZE (cm)	PROVENANCE
1849.1977[1]	Henut-tawy (*Ḥnwt-t3wy*)[2] 'Divine Adoratrice' (*dw3t-nṯr*)	Third Intermediate Period, late 21st - early 22nd Dynasty	Faience, pale blue glaze, details added in black	H. 15.5 W. 5.0 D. 4.8	Erroneously recorded as from Thebes, Deir el-Bahari, Cache I (the Royal Cache) [Probably from Thebes, the Ramesseum][3]

DESCRIPTION

Mummiform *shabti* wearing a plain tripartite wig with a *seshed* headband added in black; the arms are crossed left over right on the chest and each hand holds a hoe; a basket is shown on the rear lappet of the wig; the face is a little crude and has the eyes with brows added in black; the body of the figure has five horizontal bands of inscription giving a version of Chapter 6 of the Book of the Dead and naming the owner Henut-tawy.

The *shabti* probably came from the Third Intermediate Period cemetery found in the 19th Dynasty storerooms at the Ramesseum, site of the memorial temple of Ramesses II. By the Third Intermediate Period it is considered the temple itself was no longer a place of worship and the vast storeroom areas were considered sufficiently suitable for making into a necropolis mainly for members of the Theban priesthood, but also some princesses and Divine Adoratrices. Burial shafts and small chambers were dug, and chapels were built. The cemetery was in use until the 25th Dynasty. James Quibell excavated over 200 tombs in the late nineteenth century but only found 3 intact burials.[4]

Henut-tawy was a daughter of the 'High Priest of Amen,' Pinudjem II and his principal wife Iset-em-Khebit. She probably lived at the end of the 21st and died in the early 22nd Dynasty, hence being buried in the cemetery at the Ramesseum. Henut-tawy is only known from her *shabtis* as no other funerary equipment has ever been found. Her tomb was probably robbed by the natives of the local village of Qurna who lived on the proceeds of illicit dealing in antiquities.[5] Quibell makes no mention of Henut-tawy in the list of names he found on *shabtis* during his excavations.[6]

Maat-ka-Re (see cat. No. 9), a daughter of Pinudjem I (see cat. Nos. 6a-d), was the first 'Divine Adoratrice' of the Third Intermediate Period. Yoyotte suggests a sequence for the 'Divine Adoratrices' of the Third Intermediate Period in which Henut-tawy was the successor of Maat-ka-Ra.[7] The 'Divine Adoratice' was regarded as the most important priestesses of the Amen cult at Karnak. It may well be that the title 'Divine Adoratrice' was synonymous with that of 'God's Wife of Amen,' as found on some of the *shabtis* for Maat-ka-Re. The holder of these titles was supposedly a virgin who was perhaps involved in some temple rituals, perhaps of a sexual nature, as the earthly wife of the god Amen. Fazzini writes: '['God's Wife of Amen' was] linked to the concept of consort of Amen, serving to please the god, to help avert potential and terrible wrath, and to awaken the demiurge's amorous desires necessary to continuing daily creation and fecundity.'[8]

INSCRIPTION

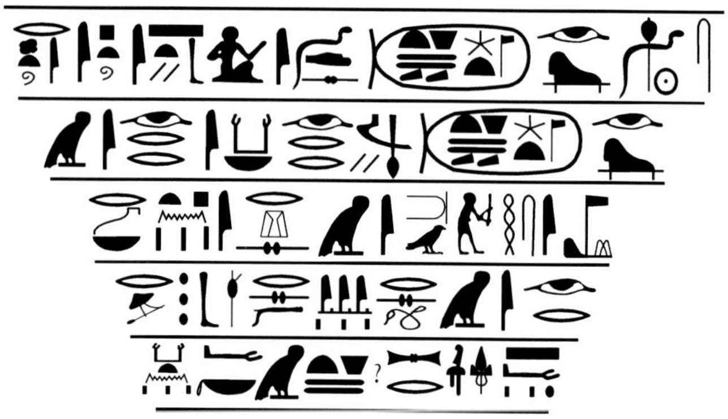

Sḥḏ Wsir dwꜣt-nṯr Ḥnwt-tꜣwy ḏd.s ỉ šbty ỉptw ỉr ḥsb tw Wsir dwꜣt-nṯr Ḥnwt-tꜣwy mꜣʿ(t)-ḫrw ỉrr(t) kꜣt nb ỉrr(t) ỉm ẖrt nṯr ỉsṯ ḥw sḏbw ỉm r ẖrt.s ỉptn r nw nb ỉr(t) ỉm r srwḏ sḫt r smḥi wḏbw r ẖnt šʿy n ỉꜣbtt (r) ỉmntt ṯs pẖr ? Ḥnwt-tꜣwy mk wi kꜣ tn

The illuminated one, the Osiris, the 'Divine Adoratrice,' Henut-tawy, she speaks: O, these *shabtis* if one counts, if one reckons the Osiris, the 'Divine Adoratrice,' Henut-tawy to do all the works which are wont to be done there in the God's land. Now indeed obstacles are implanted therewith - as a woman at her duties, you are counted off at any time to serve, to cultivate the fields, to irrigate the riparian lands, to transport by boat the sand of the East to the West and vice-versa; ? Henut-tawy, 'here I am,' you shall say.

PARALLELS

Parallels are found in Aberdeen (ABDUA 20196), Berlin (9545 & 9546),[9] Bolton (A 28.1968), Cairo (CG 48459 & 48460),[10] Cambridge (E.35.1887),[11] Chicago (9426 & 10717),[12] Cracow (XI-931 & XI-932 - an 'overseer'),[13] Dublin (1892:229 & E 72:81),[14] Florence (6584),[15] Harrogate (HARGM: 7263 - an 'overseer'),[16] Hildesheim (5482),[17] Houston, Leiden (F 1964/12.4),[18] London (BM 15763, 65803, 68934;[19] UC 39868),[20] New York (MMA 17.194.2411), Oxford (1933.1502),[21] Southport (160 & 161),[22] Stockholm, Turin (2709)[23] and Vienna (ÄS 5968).[24] Further examples are recorded in the former collections of Martyn Kennard[25] and Omar Pasha (301).[26] The Aubert collection has five shabtis, including the Omar Pasha example.[27] Other *shabtis* are known in other private collections,[28] and several more figures have been offered for sale at auctions[29] and by a dealer.[30]

1. David 1980, p. 45 no. D42 and illustration
2. Ranke 1935, PN I p. 244.12
3. Aubert & Aubert 1974, pp. 145 and 165; Aubert 1979, p. 70
4. Quibell 1898, p. 9
5. *ibid*, p. 1
6. *ibid*, plt. V
7. Yoyotte 1972, p. 50
8. Fazzini 1988, p. 4
9. Roeder 1924, p. 576
10. Newberry 1930-57, vol. 1 pp. 361-36, vol. 3 plt. XXXII
11. Budge 1893, p. 70 no. 23
12. Communication with Raymond Tindale
13. Schlögl 2000, pp. 58-59 nos. 18 & 19
14. van der Plas 2000b, CD-ROM
15. Pellegrini 1900, p. 254 no. 234
16. Communication with Dr Joann Fletcher
17. Eggebrecht 1990, pp. 70-71
18. Schneider 1977, vol. 1 pp. 97-99, vol. 2 p. 119 plt. 114, vol. 3 plt. 47 and fig. 4 no. 4.3.0.8
19. Communication with Dr John Taylor
20. Petrie 1935, p. 14 and plts. IV, XX and XXXVI no. 263
21. Communication with Dr Helen Whitehouse
22. Janes, forthcoming
23. Fabretti, Rossi & Lanzone 1881, p. 381
24. Reiser-Haslauer 1991, p. 43-44
25. Sotheby, Wilkinson & Hodge 1912, lot 690
26. Aubert 1976, p. 63
27. Aubert 1974, p. 146
28. Gosselin 2007, plts. 10a-c; Haynes 1983, pp. 13-17 nos. 6 & 7; Janes 2002, pp. 115-117 no. 58; Scott III 1992, p. 103 nos. 60B & 60C; others are known to the author in collections in Holland (2 *shabtis* including an 'overseer,' - see Thomassen 2007, p. 214) and Belgium (1 *shabti*)
29. Christie's 1984, lot 155; Sineau 1992, lot 77; Sotheby's 1992, lot 551; Sotheby's 1993, lot 146; Bonhams 1994, lot 448; Christie's 1994, lot 89; Christie's 2003a, lot 178; Christie's 2003b, lot 60; Christie's 2005, lot 139; Drouot 2006a, lot 635; Drouot 2006b lot 80, Bonhams 2006a, lot 23 - same *shabti* as Christie's 2003a & 2003b; Bonhams 2006b, lot 10; Drouot 2008, lot 479 - same *shabti* as Drouot 2006b; Drouot 2009, lot 50
30. Ede 1989, no. 42

12

MUSEUM No.	NAME(S) & TITLE(S)	DATE	MATERIAL	SIZE (cm)	PROVENANCE
1844.1977[1]	Ta-baket-Khonsu (*Tꜣ-bꜣk.t-Ḫnsw*)[2]	Third Intermediate Period, 21st Dynasty	Faience, blue glaze, details added in black	H. 10.6 W. 3.5 D. 2.5	Unknown [perhaps Thebes, Deir el-Bahari, Cache II (the Priests of Amen Cache)]

DESCRIPTION

Mummiform *shabti* wearing a plain tripartite wig with a *seshed* headband added in black; the arms are crossed left over right on the chest and the hands hold a pair of hoes modelled in shallow relief and painted black; the face is rather crude and has eyes with brows painted black; a vertical column of inscription on the front of the figure names the owner Ta-baket-Khonsu.

The *shabti* could be from Thebes, Deir el-Bahari, Cache II but all of the *shabtis* from this site known for a person with the same name are made from pottery.[3] It is a mystery why Daressy, in his list of *shabtis* found in Cache II, says the figures are made of faience.[4]

INSCRIPTION

Wsir Tꜣ-bꜣk.t-Ḫnsw mꜣꜥ(t)-ḫrw

The Osiris, Ta-baket-Khonsu, justified.

PARALLELS

No parallels appear to be known for this individual.[5]

1. David 1980, pp. 48-49 no. D36 and illustration
2. Ranke 1935, PN I p. 356.7
3. See Aubert 1998, p. 92 no. 40; Aston 2009, p. 165 - the Macclesfield *shabti* is listed but all the other examples mentioned are made of pottery
4. Daressy 1907, p. 17
5. Communication with Jean-Luc Chappaz who noted four other faience *shabtis* for Ta-baket-Khonsu but it would appear these are probably for different owners

13

MUSEUM No.	NAME(S) & TITLE(S)	DATE	MATERIAL	SIZE (cm)	PROVENANCE
1825.1977[1]		Third Intermediate Period, 21st-22nd Dynasty	Pottery	H. 9.3 W. 3.6 D. 2.3	From the Faiyum Presented by the EEF

DESCRIPTION

Mummiform *shabti* wearing a plain tripartite wig; the arms are crossed on the chest; no implements or basket appear to be indicated; below the front lappets of the wig are a small pair of breasts; the facial details are not defined but the head has large ears; the *shabti* is flat-backed; the front of the feet are missing.

1. David 1980, p. 47 no. D17

14

MUSEUM No.	NAME(S) & TITLE(S)	DATE	MATERIAL	SIZE (cm)	PROVENANCE
1832.1977[1]		Third Intermediate Period, 22nd-25th Dynasty	Faience, turquoise glaze	H. 5.7 W. 2.0 D. 1.0	Unknown [perhaps from Abydos]

DESCRIPTION

Mummiform *shabti* with hands meeting just above the waist; the figure does not appear to be wearing a wig although a headband is indicated in the modelling above the forehead; the face has a large broad nose and a wide unsmiling mouth; the eyes are small but well-defined in the modelling; the ears are not indicated; the *shabti* is flat-backed.

PARALLELS

There are parallel *shabtis* with very similar iconography in St. Helens (SAHMG 1900.010.0029 & 1900.010.0030 - recorded as coming from Abydos).

1. David 1980, p. 47 no. D24

15

MUSEUM No.	NAME(S) & TITLE(S)	DATE	MATERIAL	SIZE (cm)	PROVENANCE
1828.1977		Third Intermediate Period, 25th Dynasty	Faience, creamy white glaze (discoloured)	H. 5.6 W. 2.0 D. 1.0	Unknown [probably from Tell Nabasha][1]

DESCRIPTION

Mummiform *shabti* wearing a plain tripartite wig with short front lappets and a divine beard; the arms are not really indicated in the modelling apart from the elbows; the hands perhaps meet on the chest and carry a pair of implements indicated in shallow relief; the face is very rounded with no obvious details; the *shabti* is flat-backed.

The *shabti* is probably from Tell Nabasha based on comparable examples which have a recorded provenance. Tell Nabasha was excavated by Petrie and Griffith in 1886 for the EEF. Griffith describes the group from which this *shabti* probably derives thus: 'About 200 specimens were brought together of a broad flat shape, elbows and shoulders very prominent, the wig curved somewhat like that of Hathor, cream colour with a tinge of chocolate, the wig chocolate, the back flat, tools scarcely indicated, bearded.'

PARALLELS

Other *shabtis* with similar iconography are found in Bolton (1886.28.121.1 - recorded as coming from Tell Nabasha), Greenock (1987.440 - recorded as being excavated at Tukh el-Qaramus in 1887 by Naville and Griffith for the EEF),[2] Liverpool (3.2.87.1c - from Tell Nabasha), London (BM EA 21752, 21753, 21755, 21760 - all from Tell Nabasha, and 68667 - from Abydos; UC 40070),[3] St. Helens (SAHMG 1902.11.19 - recorded as being found by Petrie at Abydos) and Warrington (1887.41.165 - from Tell Nabasha).

Several of the parallel examples have a wig indicated in a darker glaze, usually brownish-black. Although of varying provenances perhaps the *shabtis* were made in the same workshop. Tell Nabasha and Tukh el-Qaramus are very close together in the northeastern part of the the Nile delta but Abydos is much further in distance.

1. Petrie 1888, p. 33 and plt. 1
2. Communication with George Woods
3. Petrie 1935, plt. XLI no. 508

16

MUSEUM No.	NAME(S) & TITLE(S)	DATE	MATERIAL	SIZE (cm)	PROVENANCE
1823.1977[1]	Pa-di-Iset (*Pꜣ-di-ꜣst*)[2] 'Senior of the Singers of Upper and Lower Egypt' (*ꜥꜣ ḥsy tnw šmꜥw Tꜣ-mḥw*)	Late Period, 27th-30th Dynasty	Faience, bi-chromed glaze, pale green and black	H. 8.5 W. 2.0 D. 1.6	Unknown [perhaps from Saqqara]

DESCRIPTION

Mummiform *ushabti* wearing a plain tripartite wig and a long divine beard highlighted in black glaze; the arms are crossed on the chest and the hands hold a pick in the left and a hoe in the right; there is no suggestion of a basket in the modelling; the facial details are very worn; the *shabti* has a shallow dorsal pillar with a horizontal notch indicating the bottom of the rear lappet of the wig, and stands upon a trapezoidal base; the body has two vertical columns of incised inscription, one on the front and the other on the dorsal pillar; the owner is named Pa-di-Iset.

INSCRIPTION

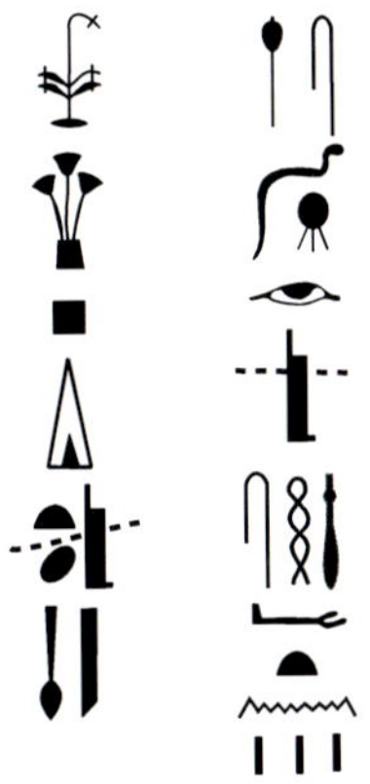

Sḥḏ Wsir ꜥꜣ ḥsy tnw šmꜥw Tꜣ-mḥw Pꜣ-di-ꜣst mꜣꜥ-ḫrw

The illuminated one, the Osiris, the 'Senior of the Singers of Upper and Lower Egypt,' Pa-di-Iset, justified.

PARALLELS

There is a parallel in Trieste (12147).[3] *Ushabtis* with similar iconography of a black wig and beard but with 'T'-shaped inscription and for different owners are found in several museums including Cairo (CG 47816-47820 for Pa-di-Ptah),[4] Cracow (A-458 for Pa-di-Ptah)[5] and Trieste (12149 & 30945 for a different Pa-di-Iset(?), 30696 & 30702 for Bak-renef).[6] See also cat. No. 17 which may be an *ushabti* for the same Pa-di-Iset although the name is written differently and it has a 'T'-shaped inscription. The title is different, perhaps suggesting an administrative role as an 'Overseer of the Singers of the [Bed]-chamber of the great House.'

1. David 1980, pp. 46-47 no. D15 and illustration
2. Ranke 1935, PN I p. 121.18
3. Tiradritti 2008, p. 184 no. 100
4. Newberry 1930-57, p. 242
5. Schlögl 2000, p. 145 no. 7
6. Tiradritti 2008, p. 184 nos. 96-99

17

MUSEUM No.	NAME(S) & TITLE(S)	DATE	MATERIAL	SIZE (cm)	PROVENANCE
1833.1977[1]	Pa-di-Iset (*Pꜣ-di-ꜣst*)[2] 'Overseer of the Singers of the [Bed]-chamber of the Great House' (*imy-r ḥsyt ny it* [*ḥnkyt*] *n Pr-ꜥꜣ*)	Late Period, 27th-30th Dynasty	Faience, bi-chrome glaze - pale green and black	H. 8.7 W. 2.4 D. 1.9	Unknown [perhaps from Saqqara]

DESCRIPTION

Mummiform *ushabti* wearing a plain tripartite wig highlighted in black glaze, and a long divine beard; the arms are crossed right over left on the chest and the right hand holds a pick and the left a hoe; no basket is carried on the back; the facial features are very well-defined, particularly the ears; the mouth has a gentle smile; the *ushabti* has a shallow dorsal pillar and stands upon a trapezoidal base; an incised 'T'-shaped inscription is filled in a black glaze; the owner is named Pa-di-Iset.

A parallel figure in Polenovo (see below) has the title translated as the 'Overseer of the Singers of the Bed-chamber of the Great House' [i.e. the Royal Palace]. Undoubtedly this is a prestigious title. Berlav and Hodjash comment that a king would be awakened and sent to sleep every day by a group of trained singers.[3] Questions must be raised as to whether the king minded having the privacy of his bedroom invaded by a group of singers. The word for bed (*ḥnkyt*) is not actually written on the *ushabti* so maybe this suggestion is a little misleading. Perhaps they sang in an anteroom to the bed-chamber. It is known that singers usually performed in groups of three or more. Presumably, as an 'overseer,' Pa-di-Iset was in charge of organising the singers, something along the lines of a manager or fixer in today's musical scene. Whether or not he actually performed is questionable as the title suggests an administrative role.

INSCRIPTION

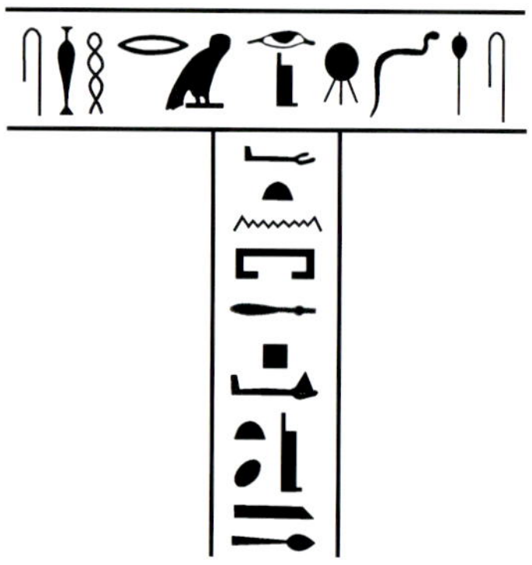

Sḥḏ Wsir imy-r ḥsyt ny it [*ḥnkyt*] *n Pr-ꜥꜣ Pꜣ-di-ꜣst mꜣꜥ-ẖrw*

The illuminated one, the Osiris, the 'Overseer of the Singers of the [Bed]-chamber of the Great House,' Pa-di-Iset, justified.

PARALLELS

A parallel is found in Polenovo (044).[4] See also cat. No. 16 which may be an *ushabti* for the same owner although with variations in the layout of the inscription, the writing of the owner's name and a different title. Further information is also given about other *ushabtis* with similar iconography under this entry.

1. David 1980, p. 47 no. D25 and illustration
2. Ranke 1935, PN I p. 121.18
3. Berlev & Hodjash 1998, pp. 105 & 296 no. 157
4. *ibid*, p. 105 no. 157 and plt. 125

18

MUSEUM No.	NAME(S) & TITLE(S)	DATE	MATERIAL	SIZE (cm)	PROVENANCE
1841.1977[1]	??-Khonsu (?) (*??-Ḫnsw ?*)	Late Period, 26th Dynasty	Faience, blue glaze	H. 2.5 W. 2.6 D. 1.6	Unknown [perhaps from Thebes, Asâsîf]

DESCRIPTION

The head and shoulders of a mummiform *ushabti* wearing a plain tripartite wig and divine beard; the face has rather puffy eyes, swollen cheeks and very large ears; the upper part of a pick is perhaps evident on the right shoulder; the cord of a basket runs over the left shoulder with the basket being carried behind; it is unclear whether a hoe is indicated on the left shoulder; the back of the wig has four horizontal bands of incised inscription; the faience is very hard, a type referred to as glassy faience.

The fragment is very similar in iconography to *ushabtis* for Ankh-Hor found at Thebes (Asâsîf, TT 414) which date from the Late Period, 26th Dynasty (see below).[2] These *ushabtis* are also made of blue glazed glassy faience, have similar facial proportions, and most have an inscription starting on the back of the wig with 'Spoken by the Osiris …' *Ushabtis* for Ankh-Hor carry a single implement, a hoe in the left hand, while the right holds the cord of a basket carried behind the left shoulder.

The inscription on the Macclesfield figure is rather crudely written and gives no obvious name (perhaps ??-Khonsu) or titles. For this reason it has been suggested this fragment is a late nineteenth century forgery, perhaps modelled on a genuine *ushabti* for Ankhor. If this is the case then it is rather strange that the forger was unable to copy the name and titles.

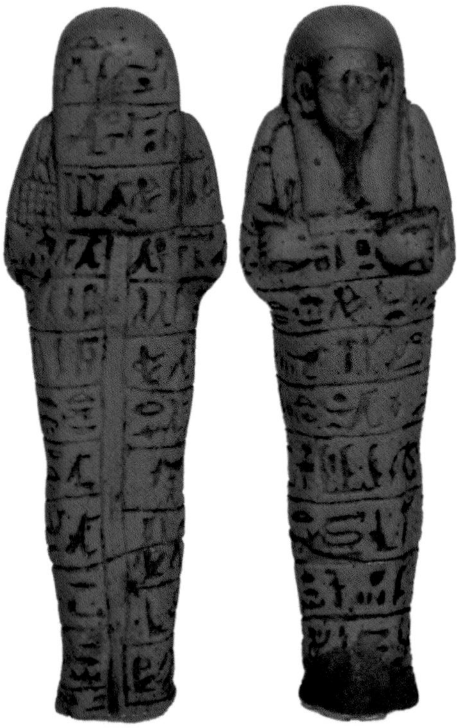

Ushabti for Ankh-Hor showing similar iconography (Janes, 2002 p. 154 no. 81)

Another owner of similar style *ushabtis* is Pa-di-Hor-resenet, also from Thebes (Asâsîf, TT 196). They are extremely rare.[3] Another similar *ushabti* with an inscription covering the entire body, including the back of the head and with an unreadable name and title, was recently sold at auction.[4] The Macclesfield fragment is most likely to be from an *ushabti* found in the Asâsîf cemetery whose name has so far not been accounted for.

INSCRIPTION

Ḏd mdw Wsir ??-Ḫnsw ??

Spoken by the Osiris, ??-Khonsu ??

1. David 1980, p. 48 no. D33 and illustration
2. For examples see Bietak & Reiser-Haslauer 1982, pts. 97-116; Janes 2002 pp. 154-155 no. 81
3. For an example see Sotheby's 1999, lot 34; see also Aubert 1974, pp. 217-218
4. Bonhams 2008, lot 15

19

MUSEUM No.	NAME(S) & TITLE(S)	DATE	MATERIAL	SIZE (cm)	PROVENANCE
1831.1977[1]	Illegible	Late Period, 26th-30th Dynasty	Faience, green glaze (gone brown)	H. 4.5 W. 1.5 D. 0.6	Unknown

DESCRIPTION

Mummiform *ushabti* wearing a plain tripartite wig and divine beard; the arms are crossed on the chest; a hoe is held in the right hand although it is only very faintly indicated in the modelling; a pick is presumed to be held in the left hand but this is also extremely faintly shown; a basket is carried behind the left shoulder; the facial details are barely discernable; the back of the *ushabti* is flat and has a vertical column of incised inscription; the lower legs and feet are missing.

INSCRIPTION

Wsir ?? ms ...?

Osiris ?? born to ....?

1. David 1980, p. 47 no. D23

20

MUSEUM No.	NAME(S) & TITLE(S)	DATE	MATERIAL	SIZE (cm)	PROVENANCE
1822.1977[1]		Late Period, 26th Dynasty	Faience, green glaze	H. 10.8 W. 2.6 D. 2.0	Unknown

DESCRIPTION

Mummiform *ushabti* wearing a plain tripartite wig and divine beard; the arms are crossed right over left on the chest and the hands hold a pick in the left and a hoe in the right; the right hand also holds the cord of a basket which is carried behind the left shoulder; the facial details are somewhat poorly-defined; the *ushabti* has a dorsal pillar with a horizontal notch indicating the bottom of the rear lappet of the wig; the figure stands upon a trapezoidal base.

1. David 1980, p. 46 no. D14 and illustration (numbered 10)

21

MUSEUM No.	NAME(S) & TITLE(S)	DATE	MATERIAL	SIZE (cm)	PROVENANCE
1815.1977[1]	Iah-mes (*Iʿḥ-ms*)[2] 'King's Scribe' (*sš nsw*) Hetep-Bastet (*Ḥtp-B3stt*)[3]	Late Period, 30th Dynasty	Faience, light turquoise glaze	H. 11.0 W. 3.0 D. 2.3	Unknown [from Giza]

DESCRIPTION

Mummiform *ushabti* wearing a plain tripartite wig and a long plaited divine beard; the arms are crossed on the chest and the hands hold a pick in the left and a hoe in the right; the right hand also holds the cord of a basket which is carried behind the left shoulder; the face, which has high cheek bones, is well-detailed and has a broad nose and a gently smiling mouth; the *ushabti* has a dorsal pillar and stands upon a trapezoidal base; the body has an incised 'T'-shaped inscription; the owner is named Iah-mes.

There are four types of *ushabtis* for this owner - small ones with either a 'T'-shaped or a vertical column of inscription, and taller ones with several bands of inscription giving a full version of Chapter 6 of the Book of the Dead - the '*Shabti* Spell.' Of the taller *ushabtis* there are two types - those with plain wigs and others with striated wigs.

Parallel examples in Leiden, London and the former Hilton Price collection have a provenance of Giza.

INSCRIPTION

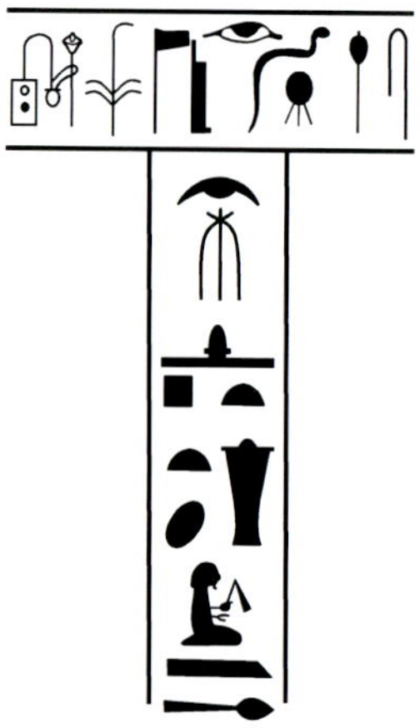

Sḥḏ Wsir sš nsw Iʿḥ-ms [ms] Ḥtp-B3stt m3ʿ-ḫrw

The illuminated one, the Osiris, the 'King's Scribe,' Iah-mes, born to Hetep-Bastet, justified.

NB - the hieroglyph *ms* is used haplographically in the owner's name and for 'born to.'

PARALLELS

Parallel examples are found in Baltimore (48.397 - tall type with a striated wig),[4] Bolton (A.50.1968, A.52.1968-A.54.1968 - all shorter type with 'T'-shaped inscription),[5] Edinburgh (NMS A.1891.43 & A.1891.44 - both tall type with striated wig, & A.1891.270 - shorter type with 'T'-shaped inscription),[6] Leiden (HD 15 & H**7 - both shorter type with a single vertical column of inscription - recorded as coming from Giza),[7] London (BM EA 71124, 71146 & 71157 - all shorter type - recorded as coming from Giza; UC 40135)[8] and Oxford (1891.0297 - shorter type with 'T'-shaped inscription, & 1961.0410 - type not known).[9] Other examples are in a private collection (shorter type with 'T'-shaped inscription)[10] and the former Hilton Price collection (shorter type with 'T'-shaped inscription - from Giza).[11]

1. David 1980, p. 46 no. D7 and illustration
2. Ranke 1935, PN I p. 12.19
3. *ibid*, PN I p. 258.4
4. Steindorf 1946, p. 162 and plts. CVI & CXIX no. 733
5. Communication with Tom Hardwick
6. Communication with Leslie-Ann Liddiard
7. Schneider 1977, vol. 2 pp. 157-158 and plt. 128, vol. 3 plt. 65 nos. 5.3.1.12 & 5.3.1.13
8. Petrie 1935, p. 15, plts. XXII and XLI no. 602
9. Communication with Dr Helen Whitehouse
10. Janes, in preparation
11. Hilton Price 1897, p. 173 no. 1642

22

	MUSEUM No.	NAME(S) & TITLE(S)	DATE	MATERIAL	SIZE (cm)	PROVENANCE
a	1812.1977[1]	Tcha-Hor-pa-ta (*Ṯ3-Ḥr-p3-t3*)[2]	Late Period, 30th Dynasty	Faience, green glaze	H. 16.8 W. 5.0 D. 2.5	Unknown [from Saqqara][5]
b	1813.1977[1]	'He who knows what exists'[3] (*si3 ntt*) 'Priest' (*ḥm-nṯr*) Tefnut (*Tfnwt*)[4]			H. 17.5 W. 5.0 D. 2.5	

1812.1977

1813.1977

DESCRIPTION

Finely-modelled mummiform *ushabtis* both wearing a plain tripartite wig and a plaited divine beard which is curled at the tip; the arms are crossed right over left on the chest; the hands hold a pick in the left and a hoe in the right, both implements are well-modelled in high relief; the right hand also holds the twisted cord of a basket which is carried behind the left shoulder; the face on both figures are well-modelled; the eyes have cosmetic lines in relief; the nose is broad with nostrils indicated; the mouth has a gentle smile, typical for the period; the *shabtis* have a dorsal pillar and stand upon a trapezoidal base; the front of the body has a vertical column of incised inscription; the owner is named Tcha-Hor-pa-ta.

This individual had two types of *ushabtis* - ones like the present examples with a vertical inscription, and others with 9 or 10 bands of horizontal inscription giving the full version of Chapter 6 of the Book of the Dead - the '*Shabti* Spell.' The latter are magnificent *ushabtis*, perhaps amongst the finest ever produced. For more on the *ushabtis* for Tcha-Hor-pa-ta see Aubert.[6] He was a very important individual who was one of Nectanebo II's most esteemed officials. His sarcophagus was discovered at Saqqara in 1911. It is made of rose granite and is in Cairo Museum (JE 29306).[7]

INSCRIPTION

1812.1977

1813.1977

Sḥḏ Wsir sꜣ ntt ḥm-nṯr Ṯꜣ-Ḥr-pꜣ-tꜣ ms Tfnwt mꜣꜥ(t)-ḫrw

The illuminated one, the Osiris, 'He who knows what exists,' the 'Priest,' Tcha-Hor-pa-ta, born to Tefnut, justified.

PARALLELS

Several parallel *ushabtis* are known. They all have a vertical column of inscription unless noted. These are found in Brussels (E.5528),[8] Cairo (47838),[9] Kaunas (Tt-2719),[10] Lausanne (Eg. 17 - horizontal bands of inscription),[11] London (BM EA 49421 & 49422), Lyon (979.3.1707 = PF.511/4),[12] Maupas (Château - two examples - upper half only of both figures - inventory numbers unknown),[13] Milan (Castello Sforzesco - two examples - upper half only of both figures - inventory numbers unknown) and Vienna (ÄS 8373 with horizontal bands of inscription & ÄS 10125).[14] Other examples have been sold at auction in Paris[15] and London.[16]

1. David 1980, p. 45 nos. D4 and D5 - both are illustrated
2. Ranke 1935, PN I p. 388.5
3. For the titles see Gauthier 1916, pp. 53-5; Perdu 1998, p. 192
4. Ranke 1935, PN I p. 380.16
5. Porter and Moss 1978, p. 504
6. Aubert 1974, p. 247-248
7. Maspero 1914, pp. 218-315 and plts. XIX-XXI
8. van der Plas (ed.) 2000
9. Newberry 1930-57, p. 247
10. Berlev & Hodjash 1998, p. 108 no. 182 and plt. 128
11. Chappaz 1984, pp. 126-128 no, 160
12. Vergnieux 1982, pp. 67-68 and plt. III no. 5.3.1.3
13. Dewachter 1985, p. 34 and plt. III
14. Written communication with Michaela Hüettner and Dr. Elfriede Haslauer; for ÄS 8373 see Brunner-Traut & Brunner 1984, p. 114 no. 91 and illustration on p. 116
15. Drouot 1989, lots 28-31 (inscription type not known) - noted by Chappaz 1990, p. 101
16. Christie's 2007, part of lot 19

23

MUSEUM No.	NAME(S) & TITLE(S)	DATE	MATERIAL	SIZE (cm)	PROVENANCE
1811.1977[1]	Pinudjem (*P3-nḏm*)[2]	Late Period, 30th Dynasty	Faience, green glaze, black paint	H. 8.0 W. 2.4 D. 1.6	Unknown

DESCRIPTION

Mummiform *ushabti* wearing a plain tripartite wig and a long divine beard which is curled at its tip; the arms are crossed on the chest; a pick is faintly indicated being held in the left hand while the hoe presumed to be held in the right hand is barely discernable; a basket is faintly indicated behind the left shoulder; the figure has a shallow dorsal pillar which has a horizontal notch delineating the bottom of the rear lappet of the wig; a vertical column of hieratic inscription is added in black on the dorsal pillar giving the name of the owner Pinudjem; the front of the feet are missing.

INSCRIPTION

Wsir P3-nḏm m3ʿ-ḫrw

The Osiris, Pinudjem, justified.

PARALLEL

There is a parallel in Bolton (1992.8.140).

1. David 1980, p. 45 no. D3
2. I am most grateful to Jean-Luc Chappaz (Geneva) for reading the inscription

24

MUSEUM No.	NAME(S) & TITLE(S)	DATE	MATERIAL	SIZE (cm)	PROVENANCE
a 1814a.1977[1]	Ipen-?? (*Ipn-??*)	Late Period, 30th Dynasty	Faience, green glaze	H. 7.6 W. 2.2 D. 1.0	Unknown [from Tell Nabasha][2] Acquired from Amelia Edwards
b 1814b.1977[1]				H. 7.6 W. 2.2 D. 1.0	

1814a.1977

1814b.1977

DESCRIPTION

Mummiform *ushabtis* wearing a plain tripartite wig and divine beard; the arms are crossed on the chest and the hands hold a pick in the left and a hoe in the right; a basket is carried behind the left shoulder; the faces are rudimentarily modelled and have bulging eyes and a faintly smiling mouth; the *ushabtis* have a shallow dorsal pillar and a large trapezoidal base. Parallel figures in London and Southport have a provenance of Tell Nabasha.

INSCRIPTION

1814a.1977

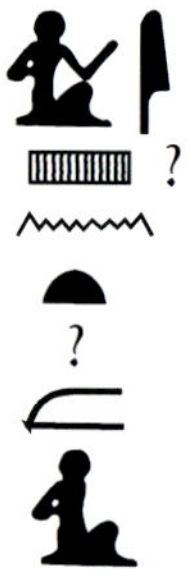

1814b.1977

Ipn-??

Ipen-??

On parallel *ushabtis* different hieroglyphs are suggested in the name of the deceased. The name clearly begins *Ipn-??* on these. Perhaps the hieroglyph ■ has been elongated on both examples in Macclesfield.

London (UC 40336) and Bolton (A.42.1966 & 1886.28.12.1).

PARALLELS

Inscribed examples are found in Bolton (A.42.1966 & 1886.28.12.1), London (BM EA 21741 & 21749 - both recorded as coming from Tell Nabasha; UC 40336 & 57158) and Southport (212 - from Tell Nabasha). Uninscribed *ushabtis* for this owner, with the same iconography, are found in Bolton (A.43.1966 - A.46.1966), London (UC 57159 & 57161) and Southport (214 - from Tell Nabasha).[3]

1. David 1980, p. 45 nos. D6a and D6b - both are illustrated
2. Griffith gives a general overview of the *shabtis* in Petrie 1888, pp. 31-33, 36-37
3. Recorded as missing

25

MUSEUM No.	NAME(S) & TITLE(S)	DATE	MATERIAL	SIZE (cm)	PROVENANCE
a 1819.1977[1]		Late Period, 30th Dynasty	Faience, dark green glaze	H. 5.3 W. 1.4 D. 1.3	Unknown
b 1839.1977[1]				H. 4.6 W. 0.8 D. 0.5	

1819.1977

1839.1977

DESCRIPTION

Mummiform *ushabtis* wearing a plain tripartite wig and divine beard; the arms are crossed on the chest; there are no signs of implements or a basket; the facial details are very rudimentary; the *ushabtis* are flat-backed and stand upon a very shallow trapezoidal base, although this is broken away in 1839.1977.

1. David 1980, pp. 46, 48 nos. D11 & D31

26

MUSEUM No.	NAME(S) & TITLE(S)	DATE	MATERIAL	SIZE (cm)	PROVENANCE
1820.1977[1]		Late Period, 30th Dynasty	Faience, green glaze	H. 5.9 W. 1.5 D. 1.4	Unknown

DESCRIPTION

Mummiform *ushabti* wearing a very stylised plain tripartite wig and divine beard (?); the arms are crossed on the chest and the hands hold a pick in the left and a hoe in the right; the facial details are very poorly defined with little attention to detail; the *ushabti* does not have a dorsal pillar although it stands upon a shallow trapezoidal base which is partly damaged.

1. David 1980, p. 46 no. D12

27

MUSEUM No.	NAME(S) & TITLE(S)	DATE	MATERIAL	SIZE (cm)	PROVENANCE
1821.1977[1]		Late Period, 30th Dynasty	Faience, green glaze	H. 6.9 W. 1.9 D. 1.3	Unknown

DESCRIPTION

Mummiform *ushabti* wearing a plain tripartite wig and divine beard; the arms are crossed on the chest and the hands hold a pick in the left and a hoe in the right although these are only just discernable; the facial details are very rudimentary; the *ushabti* is flat-backed and stands upon a small trapezoidal base.

1. David 1980, p. 46 no. D13

28

MUSEUM No.	NAME(S) & TITLE(S)	DATE	MATERIAL	SIZE (cm)	PROVENANCE
1830.1977[1]	Irt-ieru (*Ỉrt-ỉr.w*)[2] Ta-sesh(?) *Tꜣ-šs(?)*	Early Ptolemaic Period	Faience, bi-chrome, pale turquoise and blue glaze	H. 12.0 W. 3.8 D. 2.6	Unknown [perhaps from Deir Rifeh]

DESCRIPTION

Mummiform *ushabti* wearing a plain tripartite wig and divine beard; the front lappets of the wig have horizontal lines on the lower edge; the arms are crossed on the chest and the hands hold a pick in the left and a hoe in the right indicated in raised relief; the pick and right hand are damaged; a round-bottomed basket is carried behind the left shoulder although it is only faintly indicated; the shoulders are fairly high and quite square; the facial details are fairly rudimentary; the eyes have heavy lids; there is a dorsal pillar which has a horizontal notch indicating the lower edge of the back of the wig; the figure stands upon a trapezoidal base; a vertical column of inscription added in a darker blue names the owner Irt-ieru.

Parallel figures for the same owner are found in Rochdale. These are recorded as coming from Deir Rifeh in Middle Egypt, a site excavated by Petrie in 1907. However the *ushabti* has very similar iconography to cat. No. 28 although a parallel for this figure in Manchester is recorded as coming from Giza. Whether there has been some confusion over the provenances is unclear. There is also a similarity in the names on the *ushabtis*. Petrie's account of the excavations mentions both provenances in its title - Gizeh and Rifeh.[3]

INSCRIPTION

Sḥḏ Wsir Ỉrt-ỉr.w ms Tꜣ-šs(?) mꜣʿ(t)-ḫrw

The illuminated one, the Osiris, Irt-ieru, born to Ta-sesh(?), justified.

PARALLELS

There are parallels in Rochdale (89.27.1 - 89.27.4).

1. David 1980, p. 47 no. D22 and illustration
2. Ranke 1935, PN I p. 42 for similar
3. Petrie 1907

29

MUSEUM No.	NAME(S) & TITLE(S)	DATE	MATERIAL	SIZE (cm)	PROVENANCE
1838.1977[1]	Iry-r (*Ỉry.r*)[2] Seshw(?) (*Šsw*) (?)	Early Ptolemaic Period	Faience, bi-chrome, pale turquoise and blue glaze	H. 11.7 W. 3.6 D. 2.3	Unknown [perhaps from Giza]

DESCRIPTION

Mummiform *ushabti* wearing a plain tripartite wig and divine beard; the front lappets of the wig have horizontal lines on the lower edge; the arms are crossed on the chest and the hands hold a pick in the left and a hoe in the right indicated in raised relief; the right hand also holds the twisted rope for a round-bottomed basket which is carried behind the left shoulder; the facial details are fairly rudimentary but the eyes are quite large and have heavy lids; the nose is damaged; the *ushabti* has a dorsal pillar with a horizontal notch indicating the lower edge of the back of the wig, the figure stands upon a trapezoidal base; a vertical column of inscription added in a darker blue names the owner Iry-r.

A parallel in Manchester for this owner has a provenance of Giza. The *ushabti* has very similar iconography to cat. No. 27 although parallels to this example in Rochdale are recorded as coming from Deir Rifeh.

INSCRIPTION

Sḥḏ Wsir Ỉry.r ms Šsw(?) ...

The illuminated one, the Osiris, Iry-r, born to Seshw(?) ....

PARALLEL

There is a parallel in Manchester (4861).

1. David 1980, p. 48 no. D30 and illustration
2. Ranke 1935, PN I p. 42.10

30

MUSEUM No.	NAME(S) & TITLE(S)	DATE	MATERIAL	SIZE (cm)	PROVENANCE
1842.1977[1]	Djed-Hor (*Ḏd-Ḥr*)[2] 'Priest' (*ḥm-nṯr*)	Early Ptolemaic Period	Faience, deep blue glaze	H. 12.0 W. 3.8 D. 2.2	Unknown [from Abydos, Cemetery G (Tomb G 50) - the tomb of Djed-Hor - 'Priest of Hathor of Denderah'][3]

DESCRIPTION

Mummiform *ushabti* wearing a plain tripartite wig and divine beard; the arms are crossed on the chest and the hands hold a pick in the left and a hoe in the right; the right hand also holds the cord for a round-bottomed basket which is carried behind the left shoulder; the face is small and poorly defined; the ears are large and the nose is pointed; the shoulders are quite square; the *ushabti* has a shallow dorsal pillar and stands upon a small trapezoidal base; there are faint traces of inscription added in black on the front of the *ushabti*.

By comparison with similar figures in London and Manchester this is an *ushabti* for Djed-Hor, son of Wedjat-iw, from Cemetery G at Abydos (Tomb G 50 - see plan opposite). The cemetery lies between the great memorial temple of Seti I and the temple of Osiris and to the east of the processional way leading to Umm el Qa'ab, burial place of the first kings of Egypt.[4]

Djed-Hor's tomb was found undisturbed. It was excavated by Petrie in 1902. It comprises two vaulted brick chambers in which Djed-Hor was buried with other members of his family (see cat. Nos. 31, 32 and 33).

Petrie notes that '*Outside the sarcophagus* [of Djed-Hor] *at the head were two boxes of ushabtis… One box contained 198, and the other 196 figures. Beneath the western box was a great quantity of much ruder ushabtis. The better ushabtis were of fairly hard, dark, greeny-blue glaze, inscribed in ink.*'[5]

Ushabtis for Djed-Hor occur in two sizes, smaller examples like the one in the present collection, and larger ones with square, broad shoulders and generally of rather plump proportions including a broad dorsal pillar. Like the smaller examples, the larger type also carry a round-bottomed basket. The colour of the glaze on the *ushabtis* varies from deep blue to greenish-blue. Some have a lighter blue glaze.

Djed-Hor was buried in a stone sarcophagus (now in Cairo Museum, Temp. no. 15.1.21.3)[6] - B in Petrie's tomb plan. His mummy was not placed in wooden coffins within the sarcophagus but was simply lying on a wooden board. The mummy was adorned with two sets of amulets. An outer group, made of glazed faience, was found lying on the chest outside the mummy wrappings, and an inner group, made of stone, was found within the wrappings although some had become displaced from their original position.[7] The stone amulets include ones made of feldspar, haematite, red serpentine and lapis lazuli. These are now in Philadelphia.[8] A bronze *hypocephalus*, a flat amuletic disc, was found under Djed-Hor's head.[9] The *hypocephalus* is one of the rarest of amulets, only about 100 are known. It was placed under the head of the deceased to ensure eternal life by magically providing warmth and heat as noted in Chapter 162 of the Book of the Dead with which they are usually inscribed. The *hypocephalus* found beneath the head of Djed-Hor was not inscribed with his name. It is now in Cairo Museum (JE 38355; CG 3590).[10] Another one which is inscribed for him was found in the inner wooden coffin belonging to the owner of sarcophagus C in the tomb group. This *hypocephalus* is now in London (BM EA 37330).[11] A third example, now in Boston (MFA 02.766),[12] was found in sarcophagus D.

A number of the finds from Petrie's excavations at Abydos were exhibited in London at University College in 1902. These included *ushabtis*, the amulets and two of the *hypocephali* for Djed-Hor.[13]

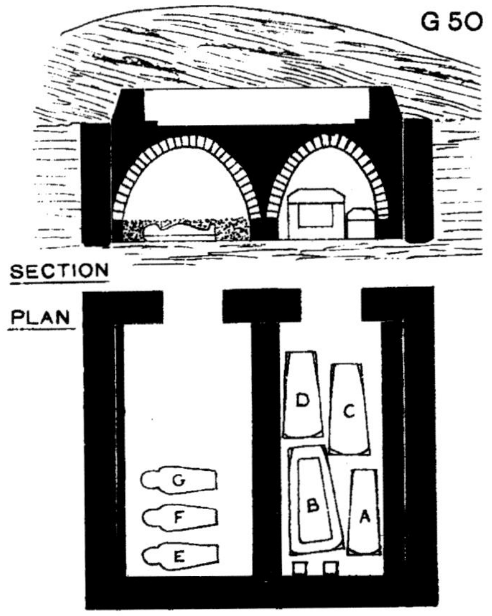

Plan of Tomb G 50 from Petrie 1902, plt. LXXX
(courtesy of the Egypt Exploration Society)

A - sarcophagus without name
B - sarcophagus for Djed-Hor (note the *ushabti* boxes drawn at the head)
C - sarcophagus - coffin without name - inscription destroyed by white ants
D - sarcophagus for Neb-ta-ahit (wife of Djed-Hor)
E - Horudja (son of Djed-Hor)
F - Pet-en-Iset (son of Djed-Hor)
G - Pet-Osiris (son of Djed-Hor - see cat. No. 31)

INSCRIPTION

Only faint traces of the inscription remain. Parallel *ushabtis* in London and Manchester give a clearer reading thus:

Ỉ wšbty ipn ir iptw Wsir ḥm-nṯr Ḏd-Ḥr

O, these *shabtis*, if one counts, the Osiris, the 'Priest,' Djed-Hor.

PARALLELS

Most of the parallels have inscriptions in varying degrees of clarity. They are found in Bolton (1902.53.35, 1902.53.37 & 1902.53.38 - smaller type - all recorded as coming from Abydos), Boston (MFA 02.780, 02.782-07.86 - smaller type, and 02.781 - larger type - all are recorded as coming from Abydos, Cemetery G, tomb G 50),[14] (Chicago (OIM 7126 & 7141 - smaller type, and 7135 - perhaps larger type - all from Abydos),[15] Edinburgh (NMS A.1902.306.11 F-I - smaller type, and A.1902.306.11 F - larger type - all recorded as coming from Abydos, cemetery G),[16] London (BM EA 37336-37337 - smaller type, and 37338 - larger type - all are recorded as coming from Abydos; UC 40162 - larger type, 40163a & b - both smaller type),[17] Manchester (1179a-h - all smaller type - recorded as coming from Abydos), Oxford (1896-1908 E.3568 - smaller type, from Abydos) and St. Helens (SAHMG 1902.11.3, 1902.11.4, 1902.11.7, 1902.11.8 & 1904.7.4 - smaller type - recorded as coming from Abydos except for the 1904.7.4).

According to distribution lists, *ushabtis* for Djed-Hor are recorded as being presented to museums in Aberdeen, Connecticut (Yale University Museum), Detroit (Museum of Art), Pittsburgh (Carnegie Museum) and Würzburg (University Museum) by the Egypt Exploration Fund (EEF) in 1902.[18] It has not been possible to obtain inventory numbers for these.

1. David 1980, p. 48 no. D34
2. Ranke 1935, PN I p. 411.12
3. Petrie 1902, pp. 37-39; Porter & Moss 1937, p. 75
4. For a general plan of the sites at Abydos see Porter & Moss 1937, p. 38; Dodson & Ikram 2008, p. 329
5. Petrie 1902, p. 38 and plt. LXXIX - 1st, 3rd & 5th figures in the group illustrated in fig. 1.
6. Malek (ed.), Magee, Fleming & Hobby 2010, p. 832
7. Petrie 1902, plt. LXXVIII. Petrie says the amulets are made of glazed pottery (?)
8. Communication with Chrisso Boulis; O'Connor & Silverman 1980, pp. 64-65 - several of the amulets are illustrated - cat. Nos. 71 & 72 (a winged scarab made of faience - PUM E11384a-c; faience amulets of Khnum, Isis, Hathor, Horus and Anubis - PUM E11386 & E11388-11391; carnelian amulets of a heart, *kheper*-bettle and a *wedjat*-eye - PUM E11397, E11405 & E11416)
9. Petrie 1902, p. 50 and plts. LXXVI & LXXIX no. 5
10. Porter & Moss 1937, p. 75; Maspero 1915, p. 361
11. Porter & Moss 1937, p. 75; Petrie 1902, plts. LXXVII & LXXIX no. 3; British Museum web site
12. Petrie 1902, plts. LXXVII & LXXIX no. 4; D'Auria, Lacovera & Roehrig 1988, p. 228 no. 183
13. Petrie 1902a, pp. 14-15 nos. 18 & 20
14. Communication with Dr Lawrence Berman
15. Communication with Susan Allison
16. Communication with Lesley-Ann Liddiard
17. Petrie 1935, p. 15, plts. XXIII and XLV nos. 646-647
18. I am most grateful to Chris Naunton of the EES who gave me access to archival material

31

	MUSEUM No.	NAME(S) & TITLE(S)	DATE	MATERIAL	SIZE (cm)	PROVENANCE
a	1816.1977[1]	[Pet-Osiris]	Early Ptolemaic Period	Faience, brilliant blue glaze	H. 9.8 W. 3.1 D. 2.5	From Abydos, Cemetery G [Tomb G 50] - the tomb of Djed-Hor ('Priest of Hathor of Denderah')[2]
b	1817.1977[1]				H. 9.8 W. 3.0 D. 2.3	Presented by the EEF
c	1840.1977[1]				H. 9.9 W. 3.1 D. 2.4	

1816.1977

1817.1977

1840.1977

DESCRIPTION

Well-modelled mummiform *ushabtis* wearing a plain tripartite wig and divine beard; note the arms are held left above right on the chest; the left hand holds a pick and the right a hoe modelled in relief; the blade of the pick, in particular, has a distinctive curve; the right hand also holds the cord of a basket which is carried behind the left shoulder; the *ushabtis* have a dorsal pillar and stand upon a trapezoidal base. The figures have a lustrous brilliant blue glaze.

Although without inscription the *shabtis* are undoubtedly for Pet-Osiris, son of Djed-Hor (see cat. No. 30), the owner of tomb G 50 in Cemetery G at Abydos. Petrie, who excavated the tomb in 1902, writes of the *ushabtis*: *'These are brightly glazed, of a brilliant light blue; some with purple wigs* [bi-chrome glazed]; *and others larger, with purple wigs and inlaid purple inscription for the priest of Hathor and Uazit* [Wedjat], *Peduasar* [Pet-Osiris] *son of Zedher* [Djed-Hor]. *The ushabtis were mixed throughout the sand around the three burials* [Horudja, Pet-en-Iset & Pet-Osiris]; *three were in the sand within the sarcophagus* G [Pet-Osiris], *the lid of which was tilted; but more than half lay in one group north of that. The total numbers were, plain 266, purple heads 83, inscribed 36; the total of 385 seems to have been originally 400, like the deposits already noticed.'*[3] It is possible the 36 examples inscribed with a version of Chapter 6 of the Book of the Dead - the '*Shabti* Spell,' are intended to be 'overseer' *ushabtis*, while those without inscription are workers.

Pet-Osiris was buried with his parents, Djed-Hor and Nebta-ahit, and two of his brothers, Horudja and Pet-en-Iset. The sarcophagus of Pet-Osiris is in Cairo Museum (no number assigned) together with others from his family.

A number of the finds from Petrie's excavations at Abydos were exhibited in London at University College in 1902. These included *ushabtis* for Pet-Osiris.[4]

PARALLELS

Many of the *ushabtis* were distributed to museums by the Egypt Exploration Fund (EEF) in 1902. 12 of the 36 inscribed examples noted by Petrie have been traced.

Parallels which are certainly for Pet-Osiris showing the hands placed one above the other on the chest, the distinctive curve on the blade of the pick and the lustrous blue glaze are found in Batley (KLMUS: 966.9 & 966.28 without inscription and 966.16 with inscription, - from Abydos),[5] Bolton (1902.53.39, 1902.53.41, 1902.53.42 & A.3.1965 - from Abydos), Boston (02.780, 02.787 & 02.788 - without inscription - recorded as coming from Abydos, Cemetery G, Tomb G 50),[6] Brussels (E.0485A-C without inscription, and E.0485E with inscription),[7] Cairo (current display number 10479 & 10477 - without inscription), Cambridge (E.272.1939 - without provenance or inscription), Chicago (OIM 7142 - with inscription, and 7156 without inscription - both are recorded as coming from Abydos),[8] Edinburgh (NMS A.1902.306.11, A.1902.306.11A-A.1902.306.11E - all six, which are without inscription, are recorded as coming from Abydos, Cemetery G.[9] The author is aware of another figure which is inscribed but the inventory number has not been ascertained), Leiden (F 1970/5.9 - with inscription - from Abydos),[10] Liverpool (16.9.02.22 - 2 uninscribed *ushabtis*; 16.9.02.23 - a group of 11 *ushabtis*, 2 with inscription & 1973.4.77. All are recorded as coming from Abydos, Cemetery G with the exception of the latter which was acquired from the Sir Henry Wellcome collection in 1973),[11] London (BM EA 37331 & 37332 with inscription, EA 37333-33735 without inscription - all are recorded as coming from Abydos, Cemetery G, Tomb G 50;[12] UC 40160 - with inscription, 40161 and 40164 without),[13] Manchester (1172a-d & 1177a-c - from Abydos, 1177c with inscription), Oxford (1896-1908 E.3565 & E.3566 - from Abydos, the latter with inscription), St. Gallen (C 3446 - without inscription or provenance),[14] St. Helens (SAHMG 1902.11.5 & 1902.11.6, without inscription - from Abydos) and Tübingen (139 - without inscription or provenance).[15] Aubert cites 6 examples in the Victoria & Albert Museum.[16] Other *ushabtis* with similar iconography have been seen for sale on the art market.[17]

According to distribution lists, *ushabtis* for Pet-Osiris are recorded as being presented to museums in Aberdeen (University Museum), Connecticut (Yale University Museum), Detroit (Museum of Art) and Pittsburgh (Carnegie Museum) by the Egypt Exploration Fund (EEF) in 1902.[18] It has not been possible to obtain inventory numbers for these.

There are other *ushabtis* in London (BM EA 34283-34288, 35106-35108 & 35393-35397 - all are without inscription) with the arms held in the same position although without the pronounced curve to the blade of the pick. They have a lighter blue glaze. They were purchased in 1901 and do not have a recorded provenance. The group is undoubtedly for another owner at Abydos as they were acquired before Petrie excavated in 1902. They are perhaps from another burial in Cemetery G. Two other *ushabtis* similar to this particular group are in Rochdale (89.27.5) and Aberdeen (ABDUA 20163). Both are without inscription or provenance and have a lighter blue glaze.

An upper-half fragment with similar iconography is in London (BM EA 47450) although this is recorded as coming from the excavations conducted by D. G. Hogarth at Asyut in 1906-1907. This *ushabti* is perhaps from the same workshop as the ones from Abydos. The British Museum also has a fine *ushabti* for Wrtyw, born to Hathor-iyti (EA 54847), which also shows the arms in the same position as seen in the Macclesfield group. No provenance is recorded for this figure. Two further *ushabtis* are known in private collections but neither have the distinctive curved pick so are undoubtedly for different owners.[19]

1. David 1980, p. 46 nos. D8 and D9 - both illustrated; p. 48 no. D32
2. Porter & Moss 1937, p. 75
3. Petrie 1902, pp. 38-39 and plt. LXXXIX. For a plan see plt. LXXX
4. Petrie 1902a, p. 15 no. 20
5. No. 966.9 reported stolen in 2005 - communication with Katina Bill
6. Communication with Dr Lawrence Berman
7. van der Plas 2000
8. Communication with Susan Allison
9. Communication with Lesley-Anne Liddiard
10. Schneider 1977, vol. 2 p. 174 & vol. 3 plt. 59 no. 5.3.1.115
11. Communication with Dr Ashley Cooke; see also Bienkowski & Southworth 1986, pp. 11-12
12. Communication with Dr John Taylor
13. Petrie 1935, p. 15 and plts. XXII & XLV nos. 645-649; for UC 40164 see Stewart 1995, p. 31 no. 32
14. Schögl & Brodbeck 1990, p. 313 no. 226
15. Brunner-Traut & Brunner 1981, p. 288; communication with Daniel von Recklinghausen
16. Aubert 1974, pp. 265-266, 282
17. Drouot 1997, lot 255 (3 *ushabtis* without inscription)
18. I am most grateful to Chris Naunton of the EES who gave me access to archival material
19. Haynes 1983, pp. 38-39; Janes 2002, p. 219 no. 113 erroneously dated to the Late Period, 26th Dynasty

32

MUSEUM No.	NAME(S) & TITLE(S)	DATE	MATERIAL	SIZE (cm)	PROVENANCE
1818.1977[1]		Early Ptolemaic Period	Faience, blue glaze	H. 13.4 W. 4.4 D. 3.3	From Abydos, Cemetery G [Tomb G 50] - the tomb of Djed-Hor -('Priest of Hathor of Denderah')[2] Presented by the EEF. Recorded as being from the tomb of Pet-Osiris

DESCRIPTION

Mummiform *ushabti* wearing a plain tripartite wig and divine beard; the front lappets have horizontal lines at the bottom; the top of the wig has a rounded and unglazed break mark perhaps caused by an adjacent *ushabti* in the firing process when the figures were placed in a kiln; the arms are crossed on the chest and the hands hold a pick in the left and a hoe in the right, both modelled in relief; there is no evidence of a basket in the modelling; the legs are indicated and also the knee-caps; the *ushabti* has a deep dorsal pillar with a horizontal notch indicating the bottom of the rear lappet of the wig, and stands upon a shallow trapezoidal base.

Although recorded as being from the tomb of Pet-Osiris (really Djed-Hor - see cat. No. 30) at Abydos this *ushabti* is different stylistically when compared to Macclesfield nos. 1816.1977, 1817.1977 and 1840.1977 in that the position of the hands is more traditional. Perhaps this is an *ushabti* for another member of Djed-Hor's family although no parallels are obvious.

1. David 1980, p. 46 no. D10
2. Porter & Moss 1937, p. 75; see also Petrie 1902, pp. 38-39

33

	MUSEUM No.	NAME(S) & TITLE(S)	DATE	MATERIAL	SIZE (cm)	PROVENANCE
a	1824.1977[1]		Early Ptolemaic Period	Pottery	H. 14.1 W. 4.0 D. 2.2	Erroneously said to be from the Faiyum [from Abydos, Cemetery G, tomb G 50][2]
b	1826.1977[1]				H. 15.8 W. 3.8 D. 2.8	Presented by the EEF

1824.1977

1826.1977

DESCRIPTION

Mummiform *ushabtis* with hands which appear to meet on the chest holding an implement(?) hanging pendant below; facial details are very rudimentary; the legs and feet are indicated; the *ushabtis* are very thin in depth and both have a slightly concave-shaped back; there are very faint finger prints on the back of both *ushabtis* where they were pressed into a mould.

PARALLELS

There are comparable *ushabtis* in London (UC 40166a-e).[3] These figures are also made of pottery, are of comparable size, and show the same hand positions and modelling of the legs. These *ushabtis* are recorded as coming from the tomb of Djed-Hor at Abydos (Cemetery G, Tomb 50 - see cat. No. 30) and are dated to the early Ptolemaic Period. Other parallel *ushabtis are* in Batley (KLMUS: 966.21 & 966.22),[4] Bolton (1902.53.36 & 1902.53.40), Greenock (1981.949 & 1981.596 - presented by the EEF),[5] Liverpool (16.9.02.27 - 3 *ushabtis*),[6] London (BM EA 37341-37345 - from Abydos) and Manchester (1182a-c - from Abydos).

1. David 1980, p. 47 nos. D16 & D18
2. Petrie 1902, pp. 37-40
3. For two of these see Petrie 1935, p. 15, plt. XLV nos. 651 & 652
4. Communication with Katina Bill
5. Communication with George Woods
6. Communication with Dr Ashley Cooke

34

MUSEUM No.	NAME(S) & TITLE(S)	DATE	MATERIAL	SIZE (cm)	PROVENANCE
a 1829a.1977[1]		Early Ptolemaic Period	Faience, turquoise blue glaze	H. 5.0 W. 1.6 D. 1.1	From Abydos, Cemetery G Presented by the EEF
b 1829b.1977[1]				H. 5.0 W. 1.6 D. 1.1	

1829a.1977

1829b.1977

DESCRIPTION

Mummiform *ushabtis* wearing a plain tripartite wig with lappets indicated at the front; the arms are crossed right over left on the chest; no implements or basket are evident in the modelling; the facial details are fairly rudimentary; the *ushabtis* are flat-backed. They are recorded as coming from Abydos, Cemetery G (see cat. No. 30 for more information).

PARALLELS

There are seven parallel *shabtis* in Manchester (1178a-g) which also have a provenance of Abydos, and there is a possible parallel in Greenock (1981.1023 - presented by the EEF).[2]

1. David 1980, p. 47 nos. D20 & D21
2. Communication with George Woods

35

MUSEUM No.	NAME(S) & TITLE(S)	DATE	MATERIAL	SIZE (cm)	PROVENANCE
1874.1977[1]	Ashakhet (*ꜥšꜣ.wt-ẖ.wt*)[2] 'Chief of the Servants' (*ḥry sḏm-ꜥš*) 'Chief of the Servants of Amen' (*ḥry sḏm-ꜥš n ꞽImn*)	New Kingdom, late 19th Dynasty	Wood, polychrome decoration	Box H. 32.0 L. 23.5 D. 16.5 Lids L. 10.0	Unknown [perhaps from western Thebes]

DESCRIPTION

This double compartment *shabti* box[3] is in a remarkably good state of preservation and is decorated with well-painted scenes. Some doubts have been raised about its authenticity which will be briefly discussed later.

Constructed of wooden panels secured with dowels, the box takes the shape of two shrines joined together, the so-called *per-nu* shrine of Lower Egypt.[4] The box is divided into two compartments by a tall central element of equal proportions to the narrow ends of the box. The compartments are closed with rounded lids. It was customary to secure lids by tying rope around knobs fitted to the sides and lids of the box but this is not the case with this example. Both compartments would have held two or three *shabtis*. The *shabtis* themselves would have been made of wood and undoubtedly equally well-painted although none are known. The box is covered in a layer of gesso providing a smooth surface upon which to add the decoration. The underlying ground colour of the box is yellow.

The iconography on the *shabti* box suggests it is from western Thebes, perhaps the cemetery at the village of Deir el-Medina. In ancient times the village was known as the 'Place of Truth' and it occupants were regarded as the most privileged in Egypt because the workmen and craftsmen were chosen for the quality of their work to excavate, build and decorate the Royal Tombs in the nearby Valley of the Kings and Valley of the Queens.

The owner of the box, Ashakhet, has the title 'Chief of the Servants' and 'Chief of the Servants of Amen.' His full title might have been 'Chief of the Servants of Amen in the Place of Truth' and as such he would have been in charge of a number of workmen known as a 'Gang in the Place of Truth.' Unfortunately Ashakhet seems unknown in the vast amount of documentation found at Deir el-Medina so the suggested provenance cannot be verified.

Side A

Side A shows the god Osiris, 'Lord of Eternity,' in his customary mummiform guise with both legs together sitting on a cube-shaped throne with a cloth thrown over the low back for added comfort. The side of the throne is decorated with alternating blue, green and red horizontal bands and the lower left corner is painted red. Osiris's tight-fitting shroud is painted blue, and he wears a jacket which is painted red with blue dot decoration. The blue dots are surrounded by rings of smaller dots in white. On his head is a white crown (*atef*) with two side plumes painted green and outlined in blue. The god holds a crook and flail, symbols of Kingship, in his hands. The face and hands of Osiris are painted green, the colour associated with resurrection. Facial details include a chin strap for a long curling beard, a mouth and an eye with brow painted black and white. The god's neck has short crease lines at the front. A broad collar is worn on his chest.

Ashakhet, the deceased owner of the *shabti* box, is shown facing Osiris with his arms raised in adoration. He wears a short bag-wig with curls indicated. His flesh is painted red with his facial details begin added in black and white. He wears a pleated skirt, painted white and decorated with a string of convolvulus leaves.[5] He wears a broad collar, armlets and bracelets. He is bare-footed. Depictions of Osiris usually show the enthroned god raised on a platform but in this scene he is on the same level as the deceased who stands before him.

Between the two figures is an offering table. Because of lack of floor space this is painted above the ground level of the scene. The offerings consist of round pomegranates(?) with a jar in the middle. Green palm leaves surround the offerings to keep them cool and fresh. A large lotus bloom, a symbol of rebirth, is shown on top of the offerings.

INSCRIPTION - side A

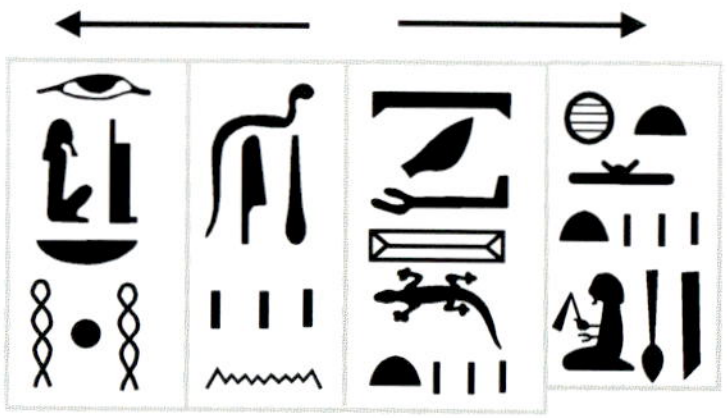

Ḏd mdw n Wsir nb nḥḥ

ḥry sḏm-ʿš ʿš3.wt-ẖ.wt m3ʿ-ḫrw

Spoken by Osiris, 'Lord of Eternity.'

The 'Chief of the Servants,' Ashakhet, justified.

Side B

Side B is decorated with a scene showing Anubis, 'Foremost of the Westerners,' seated on a cube-shaped throne similarly painted to the one used by Osiris on the opposite side of the box. Anubis is shown jackal-headed and wearing a tripartite wig painted blue with tall pointed ears projecting at the top. His face and ears are painted green, with facial details being in black and white. He wears a short kilt and holds an *ankh*, symbol of 'life,' in his right hand, and a tall *was*-sceptre, the symbol for 'dominion,' in his left. He wears a broad collar across his chest. The tail of a bull, representing virility and power, is painted in front of his legs.

Ashakhet is shown shaven-headed standing before Anubis with his arms raised in adoration. All his other details are the same as in the scene on the opposite side of the box.

Between the two figures is an offering table. This table is slightly smaller than the one shown on the other side of the box but is identical in every other aspect.

INSCRIPTION - side B

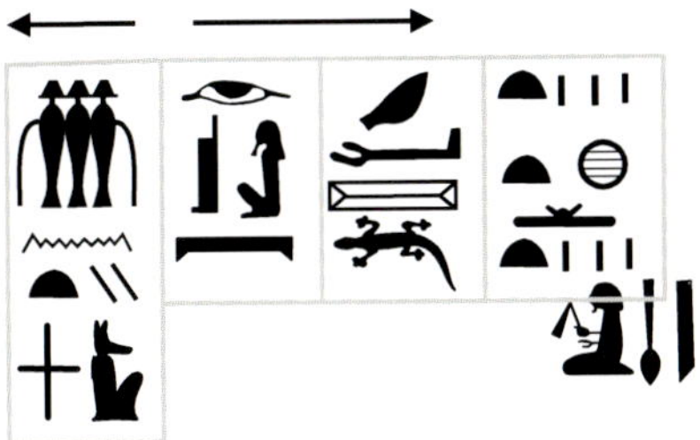

Ḫnty ỉmn-tyw ỉnpw

Wsỉr ḥry sḏm-ʿš ʿš3.wt-ḫ.wt m3ʿ-ḫrw

'Foremost of the Westerners,' Anubis.

The Osiris, the 'Chief of the Servants,' Ashakhet, justified.

End C

End D

The narrow ends of the box are painted with gods known as the Fours Sons of Horus in their capacity as guardians. Each is shown mummiform and wearing a tripartite wig. They wear short jackets painted yellow with horizontal striped decoration and have a long sash painted red with alternating white and blue dot decoration in front of them. Mummy braces, used to hold the wrappings and shroud in place on the mummy, are shown on the body of the gods.

End C shows jackal-headed Duamutef with a black face and dark blue tripartite wig and body, falcon-headed Qebsebenuef with a white face, blue tripartite wig and green body. End D shows human-headed Imsety, his face painted red and with a chin strap and long curling beard, with a dark blue body, and baboon-headed Hapi with his face also painted red but with a green body. All four deities are shown with an arm held before them painted red.

At the top of each end panel is a geometric frieze, painted blue, green, yellow, red and white with vertical lines added in black, above which is a large *wedjat*-eye, a symbol of wholeness.

INSCRIPTION - ends C & D

Wsir nb nḥḥ ḥḳ3 ʿnḫ ḏt

Dw3-mwt.f nṯr ʿ3 ẖsr Ḳbḥ-snw.f nṯr ʿ3 ẖsr nty

Osiris, the 'Lord of Eternity,' the 'Ruler,' living forever

The 'Great God,' Duamutef, dispels [evil], and the 'Great God,' Qebsebenuef, dispels [evil].

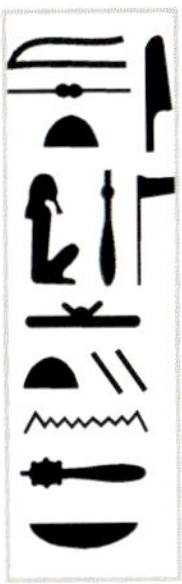

Ḥpy nṯr ˁ3 ẖsr

Hapi, the 'Great God,' dispels [evil].

ỉmstˁ nṯr ˁ3 ẖsr nb

The 'Great God,' Imsety, dispels all [evil].

Lid A

Lid B

The vaulted lids, which are positioned transversely across the two compartments of the box, are inscribed with the title and name of the owner. On both, the column of inscription is flanked by rectangular panels added in green, yellow and blue. The ends of the lids are decorated with semicircular bands painted in the same colours. One end of the lids has five bands while the opposite end has only four bands. The reason for this difference is unclear.

INSCRIPTION - lids A & B

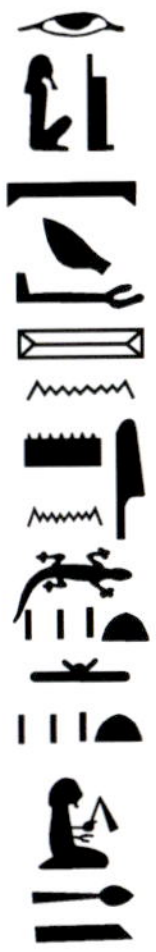

Lid A

Lid B

Wsir ḥry sḏm-ˁš n ỉmn ˁš3.wt-ḫ.wt m3ˁ-ḫrw

The Osiris, the 'Chief of the Servants of Amen,' Ashakhet, justified.

Wsir ḥry sḏm-ˁš n ỉmn ˁš3.wt-(n)-ḫ.wt m3ˁ-ḫrw

The Osiris, the 'Chief of the Servants of Amen,' Ashakhet, justified.

As mentioned above, doubts have been raised about the authenticity of the *shabti* box. Unfortunately there are no records extant that give any information as to how, where or when the box was acquired by Marianne Brocklehurst. There are perhaps certain iconographical oddities that need clarification. These include the strands of convolvulus leaves on the dress of the deceased, and the somewhat haphazard way in which some of the inscriptions are written. In three instances the text spills outside the text panels.

A *shabti* box for the 'Chantress of Amen,' Mery-Amen-dua in Philadelphia (PUM L-55-23 a-c with three *shabtis* nos. L-55-18 -19, -20 & -22)[6] shows the deceased wearing a dress decorated with a long string of convolvulus or clematis leaves. Similar *shabti* boxes are found in Berlin (733 - Pa-en-Renenutet crouching on one knee in adoration with his hands holding long strands of a similar plant before Osiris and Re-Horakhty),[7] Paris (Louvre N 2640 - for Wabet)[8] and also in Turin.

Similar text spills can be seen on a *shabti* box in Boston (1984.411).[9] Perhaps it is indicative of careless work by the scribe.

Attention has already been drawn to the fact that the Macclesfield box is unusual in that it does not have any knobs for securing the lids. It was normal to secure lids by tying rope or cord around projecting knobs on both the lid and sides of a *shabti* box.

The box may have had some areas repainted but without scientific investigation this is difficult to ascertain.

If the *shabti* box is not ancient, the forger must have had a very good understanding and knowledge of Egyptian names - Ashakhet is certainly not a common name. It is found on a statue of the goddess Renenutet in Cairo (CG 42138) - a '*wab*-priest' called Ashakhet, born to Khonsu-mes, dedicated the statue.[10] It came from the Karnak cachette and dates from the New Kingdom, 18th Dynasty. There is a 19th Dynasty Theban tomb (TT 174)[11] for another Ashakhet who has the title of 'Priest in front of Mut.'

1. David 1980, pp. 24-25 no. E24 and illustration
2. Ranke 1935, PN I p. 71.12
3. Aston 1994, pp. 24-25, 44
4. Wilkinson 1992, pp. 142-143
5. For a discussion on the identification of trailing plants see Manniche 1989, pp. 160-162
6. O'Connor & Silverman 1980, p. 42 no. 43
7. Aston 1994, p. 51 fig. 1; Kaiser 1967, p. 90 no. 926 and plt.; Roeder 1924, pp. 288-289 for the inscription
8. Bovot 2003b, pp. 40 & 81 cat. No. 2
9. D'Auria, Lacovara & Roehrig 1988, p. 156 no. 106
10. Legrain 1906, pp. 88-89
11. Porter & Moss 1960, p. 281

Chronology

NEW KINGDOM 1570-1070 BC

18th Dynasty • 1570-1293

19th Dynasty • 1293-1185

20th Dynasty • 1185-1070

THIRD INTERMEDIATE PERIOD 1069-525 BC

21st Dynasty • 1080-945 BC

(PRIEST-KINGS at THEBES - 1080-945 BC KINGS at TANIS - 1069-945 BC)

22nd Dynasty (Libyan at Tanis) • 945-715 BC

23rd Dynasty (Libyan Anarchy at Leontopolis) • 818-715 BC

24th Dynasty (Sais) • 727-715 BC

25th Dynasty (Nubian/Kushite) • 747-656 BC

LATE PERIOD 664-332 BC

26th Dynasty • 664-525 BC

27th Dynasty • 525-404 BC

28th Dynasty • 404-399

29th Dynasty • 399-380 BC

30th Dynasty • 380-343 BC

31st Dynasty • 343-332 BC

MACEDONIAN KINGS 332-305 BC

PTOLEMAIC DYNASTY 305-30 BC

Based on P. A. Clayton, *Chronicles of the Pharaohs - The Reign-by-Reign Record of the Rulers and Dynasties of Ancient Egypt* (London, 1994)

Indices

1. Royal names

2. Non-royal names

3. Royal names, transliterations

4. Non-royal names, transliterations

5. Titles

6. Titles, transliterations

7. Provenances

Concordance

Museum Number	David cat. No. (1980)	Janes cat. No. (2010)
1809.1977	D1	10
1810.1977	D2	5
1811.1977	D3	23
1812.1977	D4	22a
1813.1977	D5	22b
1814a.1977	D6a	24a
1814b.1977	D6b	24b
1815.1977	D7	21
1816.1977	D8	31a
1817.1977	D9	31b
1818.1977	D10	32
1819.1977	D11	25a
1820.1977	D12	26
1821.1977	D13	27
1822.1977	D14	20
1823.1977	D15	16
1824.1977	D16	33a
1825.1977	D17	13
1826.1977	D18	33b
1827.1977	D19	7
1828.1977	not in catalogue	15
1829a.1977	D20	34a
1829b.1977	D21	34b
1830.1977	D22	28
1831.1977	D23	19
1832.1977	D24	14
1833.1977	D25	17
1834.1977	D26	2
1835a.1977	D27a	3a
1835b.1977	D27b	3b
1836a.1977	D28a	3c
1836b.1977	D28b	3d
1837.1977	D29	4
1838.1977	D30	29
1839.1977	D31	25b
1840.1977	D32	31c
1841.1977	D33	18
1842.1977	D34	30
1843.1977	D35	8a
1844.1977	D36	12
1845.1977	D37	8b
1846.1977	D38	6a
1847.1977	D39	6b
1848a.1977	D40	6c
1848b.1977	D41	6d
1849.1977	D42	11
1850.1977	D43	9
1874.1977	E24	35
1894.1977	H5	1

Abbreviations & Bibliography

LIST OF ABBREVIATIONS

ABDUA	University of Aberdeen, Marischal Museum
ASAE	*Annales du Service des Antiquitiés de l'Égypte* (Cairo)
BIFAO	*Bulletin de l'Institute Français d'Archéologie Oriental du Caire* (Cairo)
BM	British Museum, London
BSEG	*Bulletin de la Société d'Égyptologie, Genéve* (Geneva)
BSFE	*Bulletin de la Société Française d'Égyptologie* (Paris)
BTNRP	Brighton Museum and Art Gallery
CAA	Corpus Antiquitatum Aegyptiacarum
CdE	*Chronique d'Égypte* (Brussels)
CG	*Catalogue Général des Antiquités Egyptiennes du Musée du Caire*
CMNH	Carnegie Museum of Natural History, Pittsburg
EEF	Egyptian Exploration Fund
EM	Etnografisk Museum, Oslo
GM	*Göttingen Miszellen* (Göttingen)
HARGM	Royal Pump Room Museum, Harrogate
JE	Journal d'Entree, Cairo Musuem
JEA	*Journal of Egyptian Archaeology* (London)
KLMUS	Kirklees Museums and Galleries
MFA	Museum of Fine Arts, Boston
MMA	Metropolitan Museum of Art, New York
NMS	National Museum of Scotland, Edinburgh
OIM	Oriental Institute Museum, University of Chicago
OMRO	*Oudheidkundige Mededelingen uit het Rijksmuseum van Oudheden te Leiden* (Leiden)
PUM	The University Museum, University of Pennsylvania
SAHMG	St. Helen's Museum of Glass (World of Glass)
SGL	Sociedade de Geografia de Lisboa (Lisbon)
S.R.	Special Register, Cairo Museum
RdE	*Reveue d'Egyptologie* (Leuven)
TT	Theban Tomb
UC	University College, London (Petrie Museum)

BIBLIOGRAPHY

Araújo, L. M. de

2003 *Estatuetas Funerárias Egípcias da XXI Dinastia* (Lisbon, 2003)

Aston, D. A.

1994 *'The Shabti Box - A Typological Study'* OMRO 74, (Leiden, 1994)

2009 *Burial Assemblages of Dynasty 21-25; Chronology - Typology - Developments* (Vienna, 2009)

Aubert, J. -F. & L. Aubert

1974 *Statuettes Égyptiennes - Chaouabtis, Ouchebtis* (Paris, 1974)

Aubert, J. -F.

1974 *'Une statuette de la grand prêtresse Nesikhonsou au Musée de Neuchâtel'* - Gymnase Cantonal de Neuchatel 1873-1973 (Neuchatel, 1974)

1976 *'Les statuettes funéraires de la collection Omar Pacha'* - CdE vol. 50 (Brussels, 1976)

1979 *'Chronique - Chaoubtis, chabtis et ouchebtis'* - CdE vol. 54 no. 107 (Brussels, 1979)

Aubert, L.

1987 *Tanis - L'or des pharaons* (Paris, 1987)

1998 *Les statuettes funéraires de la Deuxième Cachette à Deir el-Bahari* (Paris, 1998)

Badaway, A.

1978 *The Tomb of Nyhetep-Ptah at Giza and the Tomb of 'Ankhm'ahor at Saqqara* (Berkeley, Los Angeles and London, 1978)

Berman, L. & Bohac. K. J.

1999 *The Cleveland Museum of Art - Catalogue of Egyptian Art* (Cleveland, 1999)

Berlav, O. & Hodjash, S.

1998 *Catalogue of the Egyptian Monuments of Ancient Egypt from the Museums of the Russian Federation, Ukraine, Bielorussia, Caucasus, Middle Asia and the Baltic States* (Göttingen, 1998)

Bienkowski, P. & Southworth, E.

1986 *Egyptian Antiquities in the Liverpool Museum I - A List of the Provenanced Objects* (Warminster, 1986)

Bietak, M & Reiser-Haslauer, E.

1982 *Das Grab des 'Anch-Hor* II (Vienna, 1982)

Blackman, A.

1924 *Rock Cut Tombs of Meir* IV (London, 1924)

Bonhams

1994a *Fine Antiquities* (London, 5th July, 1994)

1994b *Fine Antiquities - Express sale system* (London, 6th December, 1994)

2006a *Antiquities* (London, 27th April, 2006)

2006b *Antiquities* (London, 13th October, 2006)

2008 *Antiquities* (London, 1st May, 2008)

2009 *Antiquities* (London, 28th, October)

Botti, G.

1955 *'Le antichità egiziane raccolte nel Museo dell'Accademia Etrusca di Cortona'* - Annurio XI (Cortona, 1955)

Bovot, J. -L.

2003a *Les serviteurs funéraires royaux et princiers de l'Ancienne Égypte* (Paris, 2003)

2003b *Chaouabtis - Des travailleurs pharaoniques pour l'éternité* (Paris, 2003)

Brunner-Traut, E. & Brunner, H.

1981 *Die Ägyptische Sammlung der Universität Tübingen* (Mainz, 1981)

1984 *Osiris, Kreuz und Halbmond - Die drei Religionen Ägyptens* (Mainz, 1984)

Budge, E. A. W.

1893 *A Catalogue of the Egyptian Collection in the Fitzwilliam Museum, Cambridge* (Cambridge, 1893)

Chappaz, J. -L.

1984 *Les Figurines Funéraires Égyptiennes du Musée d'Art et d'Histoire et de Quelques Collections Privées* (Geneve, 1984)

1990 *'Repertoire Annuel des Figurines Funeraires 3'* - BSEG 14 (Geneva, 1990)

Christie's

1984 *Antiquities* (London, 11th July, 1984)

1994 *Fine Antiquities* (London, 6th July, 1994)

1998 *Antiquities* (London, 8th April, 1998)
1999 *Antiquities* (New York, 4th June, 1999)
2001 *Antiquities* (New York, 6th December, 2001)
2003a *Antiquities including an English Private Collection of Ancient Gems, Part II* (London, 29th October, 2003)
2003b *Antiquities* (New York, 11th December, 2003)
2005 *Antiquities including property from the Leo Mildenberg collection* (London, 20th April, 2005)
2007 *Antiquities* (London, 25th October, 2007)

Cihó, M.
1984 *'Nesj-Amun's shabti from Bucarest'* - GM 72 (Göttingen, 1984)

Clayton, P.
1994 *Chronicle of the Pharaohs* (London, 1994)

D'Auria, S., Lacovara, P. & Roehrig, C.
1988 *Mummies & Magic - The Funerary Arts of Ancient Egypt* (Boston, 1988)

Daressy, G.
1907 *'Les cercueils des prêtres d'Ammon'* ASAE 8 (Cairo, 1907)
1909 *Cercueils des Cachettes Royales* (Cairo, 19009)

David, R.
1980 *The Macclesfield Collection of Egyptian Antiquities* (Warminster, 1980)

Dewachter, M.
1985 *'L'Égypte dans les Musées, Châteaux, Bibliothèques et Sociétés savantes de Province'* BSFE 103 (Paris, 1985)

Dodson, A. & Hilton, D.
2004 *The Complete Royal Families of Ancient Egypt* (London, 2004)

Dodson, A. & Ikram, S.
2008 *The Tomb in Ancient Egypt* (London, 2008)

Drouot
1989 *Vente Videau* (Paris, 24th April, 1989)
1997 *Archéologie - provenant des Collections Koutoulakis, Krief, Maspéro, Brugsch-Pasha (2e partie) et à divers amateurs* - Ricqles (Paris, 29th-30th September, 1997)
2006a *Archéologie, Arts d'Orient, Extrême-Orient* - Bergé (Paris, 28th October, 2006)
2006b *Art du Gandhâra, Archéologie, Art Islamique* - Rogeon (Paris, 9th December, 2006)
2008 *Arts d'Orient, Extrême-Orient, Archéologie* - Bergé (Paris, 29th May, 2008)
2009 *Archéologie* - Pescheteau-Badin (Paris, 12th October, 2009)

Edwards, A. B.
1883 *'Relics from the tomb of the priest-kings at Dayr-el-Baharee' - Recueil de Travaux Rélatifs à la Philologie et à l'Archéologie Égyptiennes et Assyriennes* (Paris, 1883)

Ede Ltd., C.
1989 *Small sculpture from Ancient Egypt XVI* (London, 1989)

Eggebrecht, A. (ed.)
1990 *Suche nach Unsterblichkeit - Totenkult und Jenseitsglaube im Alten Ägypten* (Mainz, 1990)

Eigner, D.
1984 *Die Monumentalen Grabbauten der Spätzeit in der Thebanischen Nekropole* (Vienna, 1984)

Erman, A. & Grapow, H.
1926-63 *Wörterbuche der Ägyptischen Sprache* (Leipzig and Berlin, 1926-1963)

Eternal Egypt
1990 *Eternal Egypt - Bes* (London, 1990)

Fabretti, A., Rossi, F., & Lanzone, R. V.
1881 *Regio Museo di Torino* (Turin, 1881)

Faulkner, R.
1981 *A Concise Dictionary of Middle Egyptian* (Oxford, 1981)

Fazzini, R.
1988 *Egypt - Dynasty XXII-XXV* (Leiden, 1988)

Forbes, D. C.
1998 *Tombs, Treasures, Mummies - Seven Great Discoveries of Egyptian Archaeology* (Sebastopol, 1998)

Gauthier, H.
1914 *Le Livres des Rois d'Égypte* vol. 3 (Cairo, 1914)
1916 *'Ziharpto, Fonctionnaire de Nectanebo I'* BIFAO 12 (Cairo, 1916)

Gabolde, M.
1990 *Catalogue des Antiquités Égyptiennes du Musée Joseph Déchelette* (Roanne, 1990)

Gosselin, L.
2007 *Les Divines Épouses d'Amon* (Paris, 2007)

Grenier, J. -C.
1996 *Les statuettes funéraires du Museo Gregoriano Egizio* (Rome, 1996)

Haan, N. de
2009 *'The search for the missing shabtis of Princess Maat-ka-ra'* - GM 220 (Göttingen, 2009)

Haynes, J.
1983 *Privately Owned Egyptian Antiquities in Ontario* - Fascicle I (Toronto, 1983)

Hilton Price, F. G.
1897 *A Catalogue of the Egyptian Antiquities in the Possession of F. G. Hilton Price, Dir.S.A.* (London, 1897)

Hope, C.
1988 *Gold of the Pharaohs* (Sydney, 1988)

Janes, G.
2002 *Shabtis - A Private View. Ancient Egyptian funerary statuettes in European private collections* (Paris, 2002)

Kaiser, W.
1967 *Ägyptisches Museum Berlin* (Berlin, 1967)

Legrain, G.
1906 *Statues et Statuettes de Rois et de Particuliers* vol. 1 (Cairo, 1906)

Lipinska, J.
1993-94 *'Bab el-Gasus - Cache-Tomb of the Priests and Priestesses of Amen'* - KMT vol. 4 no. 4 (San Francisco, 1993-94)

Malek, J. (ed.) et al.
2010 *Topographical Bibliography* - Electronic resources. *Cairo, Egyptian Museum;* http://www.griffith.ox.ac.uk/gri/3cairo.pdf

Manniche, L.
1989 *An Ancient Egyptian Herbal* (London, 1989)

Maspero, G.
1883 *Guide du visiteur au musée de Boulaq* (Paris, 1883)
1915 Guide to the Cairo Museum (Cairo, 1915)
1914 *Sarcophages des époques Persane et Ptolémaïque* (Cairo, 1914)

Mogensen, M.
1918 *Inscriptions hiéroglyphiques du musée nationale de Copenhague* (Copenhagen, 1918)

Naguib, S. A.
1985 *Funerary Statuettes* CAA (Mainz am Rhein, 1985)
1990 *Le clergè fèminin d'Amon thèbain* (Louvain, 1990)

Naville, E.
1886 *Das ägyptische Todtenbuch der XVIII. Bis XX. Dynastie* (Berlin, 1886)

Newberry, P.
1893 *Beni Hasan* I (London, 1893)
1930-57 *Funerary Statuettes and Model Sarcophagi* (Cairo, 1930-57)

Niwinski, A.
1984 *'The Bab el-Gusus Tomb and the Royal Cache at Deir el-Bahri'* - JEA 70 (London, 1984)
1988 *21st Dynasty coffins from Thebes* (Mainz, 1988)
1989 *Studies on the Illustrated Theban Funerary Papyri of the 11th and 10th Centuries B. C.* (Göttingen, 1989)
1996 *La Seconde Trouville de Deir el-Bahari (Sarcophages)* (Cairo, 1996)

O'Connor, D. & Silverman, D.
1980 *The Egyptian Mummy - Secrets and Science* (1980, Philadelphia)

Parke-Bernet Galleries, Inc.
1970 *Antiquities* (New York, 24th - 25th April 1970)

Patch, D. C.
1990 *Reflections of Greatness - Ancient Egypt at the Carnegie Museum of Natural History* (Pittsburgh, 1990)

Partridge, R. B.
1994 *Faces of Pharaohs - Royal Mummies and Coffins from Ancient Thebes* (London, 1994)

Petrie, W. M. F.
1888 *Tanis* Part II - *Nebesheh (AM) and Defenneh (Tahpanhes)* - with Chapters by A. S. Murray and F. Ll. Griffith (London, 1888)
1902 *Abydos* I - with Chapter by A. E. Weigall (London, 1902)
1902a *Catalogue of Egyptian Antiquities found by Prof. Flinders Petrie at Abydos, and Drs. Grenfell and Hunt in the Faiyum, (Egypt Exploration Fund), and drawings from the temple of the Kings (Sety I), (Egypt Research Account), 1902* July 1st - 26th (London, 1902)
1907 *Gizeh and Rifeh* (London, 1907)
1935 *Shabtis* (London, 1935)

Pellegrini, A.
1900 '*Statuette Funerarie del Museo Archeologico di Firenze*' - Bessarione vol. 7 Anno 4, Rome, 1900

Perdu, O.
1998 '*Le «Directeur des Scribes du Conseil»*' RdE 49 (Leuven, 1998)

Perdu, O. & Rickal, E.
1994 *La collection égyptienne du musée de Picardie* (Paris, 1994)

Pischikova, E.
2009 '*The Lost Necropolis of South Asasif at Luxor*' in *Ancient Egypt Magazine* vol. 9 no. 5 Issue 53 (Manchester, 2009)

van der Plas, D. (ed.)
2000 *Egyptian Treasures in Europe* vol. 2 *Musée Royeux d'Art et d'Histoire Bruxelles* CD-ROM (Utrecht, 2000)
2000b *Egyptian Treasures in Europe* vol. 3 *National Musuem of Ireland* CD-ROM (Utrecht, 2000)

Porter, B. & Moss. R.
1937 *Topographical Bibliography of Ancient Egyptian Hieroglyphic Texts, Reliefs and Paintings* - V *Upper Egypt: Sites* (Oxford, 1937)
1960 *Topographical Bibliography of Ancient Egyptian Hieroglyphic Texts, Reliefs, and Paintings* I. *The Theban Necropolis* pt. 1, *Private Tombs* Oxford, 1960)
1964 *Topographical Bibliography of Ancient Egyptian Hieroglyphic Texts, Reliefs, and Paintings* I. *The Theban Necropolis* pt. 2, *Royal Tombs and Smaller Cemeteries* (Oxford, 1964)
1972 *Topographical Bibliography of Ancient Egyptian Hieroglyphic Texts, Reliefs, and Paintings* II. *Theban Temples* (Oxford, 1973)
1978 *Topographical Bibliography of Ancient Egyptian Hieroglyphic Texts, Reliefs and Paintings* - III *Memphis* Part 2 *Saqqara to Dashur* (Oxford, 1978)

Quibell, J. E.
1898 *The Ramesseum* (London, 1898)

Ranke, H.
1935 *Die Ägyptischen Personennamen* I (Glückstadt, 1935)

Reeves, C. N.
1989 *Ancient Egypt at Highclere Castle* (Highclere Castle, 1989)
1990 *Valley of the Kings* (London, 1990)

Reeves, C. N. & Taylor, J.
1992 *Howard Carter before Tutankhamun* (London, 1992)

Reiser-Haslauer, E.
1991 *Uschebti* II (Mainz, 1991)

Roeder, G.
1924 *Aegyptische Inschriften aus den Staalichen Museen zu Berlin* vol. 2 (Berlin, 1924)

Saleh, M. & Sourouzian, H.
1987 *The Egyptian Museum, Cairo* (Mainz, 1987)

Sandman, M.
1930 '*Les Statuettes funéraires du Musée de Victoria à Upsala*' Sphinx XXII Fasc. III (Uppsala & Stockholm, 1930)

Schlögl, H.
2000 *Corpus der Ägyptischen Totenfiguren der Öffentlichen Sammlungen Krakaus* (Carcow, 2000)

Schlögl, H. & Bordbeck, A.
1990 *Ägyptische Totenfiguren aus Öffentlichen und Privaten Sammlungen der Schweiz* (Göttingen, 1990)

Schneider, H. D.
1977 *Shabtis - An Introduction to the History of Ancient Egyptian Funerary Statuettes with A Catalogue of the Collection of Shabtis in the National Museum of Antiquities at Leiden* (Leiden, 1977)

Scott III, G. D.
1992 *Temple, Tomb and Dwelling: Egyptian Antiquities from the Harer Family Trust Collection* (San Bernardino, 1992)

Sineau, A.
1992 *Archéologie Méditérranéenne* (Auxerre, 24th October, 1992)

Smith, G. E.
1912 *The Royal Mummies* (Cairo, 1912)

Sotheby's
1991 *Antiquities* (London, 8th July, 1991)
1992 *Antiquities* (London, 9th-10th July, 1992)
1993 *Antiquities* (London, 8th July, 1993)
1999 *The Christos G. Bastis Collection* (New York, 9th December, 1999)
2007 *Antiquities* (New York, 5th December, 2007)

Sotheby Wilkinson & Hodge
1911 *Catalogue of the Important and extensive Collection of Egyptian Antiquities - the property of the late F. G. Hilton-Price, Esq.* (London, 20th July, 1911)
1912 *Catalogue of the Important Collection of Egyptian Antiquities formed by the late H. Martyn Kennard, Esq.* (London, 17th July 1912)

Steindorff, W.
1946 *Catalogue of the Egyptian Sculpture in the Walters Art Gallery* (Baltimore, 1946)

Stewart, H. M.
1995 *Egyptian Shabtis* (Princes Risborough, 1995)
2000 *'Note on an enigmatic shabti form'* - JEA 86 (London, 2000)

Stuart, V.
1882 *The Funeral Tent of an Egyptian Queen* (London, 1882)

Thomassen, J.
1993 *'Egyptische dodenbeeldjes' - kunst & antikRevue* vol. 14 no. 7 May/June (Den Haag, 1993)
2007 *Zwendel in de kunst- en antiekhandel* (Soesterberg, 2007

Tiradritti, F.
1998 (ed.) *The Cairo Museum Masterpieces of Egyptian Art* (London, 1998)
2008 *Egyptian Renaissance - Archaism and the Sense of History in Ancient Egypt* (Budapest, 2008)

Vergnieux, R.
1982 *'Les Figurines Funéraires Égyptiennes du Musée Guimet d'Histoire Naturelle de Lyon' Nouv. Arch. Mus. Hist. Nat. Lyon.* Fasc. 20 suppl. (Lyon, 1982)

Wilkinson, R.
1992 *Reading Egyptian Art* (London, 1992)
2003 *The Complete Gods and Goddesses of Ancient Egypt* (London, 2003)

Yoyotte, J.
1972 *'Les Adoratrices de la IIIe Période Intermédiaire, à propos d'un chef-d'oeuvre rapporté par Champollion'* - BSFE 64 (Paris, 1972)